On Loan from the Lord

Memoir of the Life and Ministry of J.D. Seibert

By Erika Seibert

www.thisthornyrose.com

Cover Design: Stephen J. Melniszyn

Interior Design: John manning

Cover Photo: Jim Phillipps

Author Photo: Lukas and Suzy VanDyke

ISBN: 9781987436105

Dedication

First and foremost, I dedicate this book to the Lord, who graciously lent us Josh for a season. "And he said, 'Naked I came from my mother's womb, and naked shall I return. The LORD gave, and the LORD has taken away; blessed be the name of the LORD'" (Job 1:21). God has done amazing work through the life, death, and legacy of this man devoted to His service.

The book is secondly, a tribute to that amazing man, Josh Seibert. It is a loving memory of one of the most heroic men I've had the privilege of knowing personally in this life. He was a man who exemplified Christ in the flesh to me as a husband, pastor, and friend, with his last dying breath.

Then, the book is a gift to our two precious boys, Noah and Nathan, who have some big shoes to fill. It is also a tear-filled labor of love dedicated to our family and friends, the churches we've been blessed to be a part of, and the countless others serving the Lord in ministry.

May God use our testimony to inspire others to live to the fullest purpose in the Lord, even if faced with seeming tragedy, pain, suffering, or the unexpected death of a loved one. It is my prayer that God would use the testimony of His work in our lives to build up the church at large. May the story of Josh's life and ministry bring glory to God, proclaim the gospel, and edify the church. It would be Josh's wish.

By all earthly standards, Josh Seibert died too soon. However, in *On Loan from the Lord*, his wife, Erika, recounts the goodness and kindness of the Lord both in life and in death. Beautifully punctuated with letters, poems, and narrative, Erika captures the essence of their marriage together, giving light to the most intimate aspects of life, love, and ministry. This book is moving and powerful, sweet and sad, devotional and worshipful. It is a marvelous testimony to God's grace, and the amazing labor of love from a wife to her husband.

—**Nate Pickowicz**, pastor, Harvest Bible Church, Gilmanton Iron Works, NH.

Your sons will take the place of your fathers; you will make them princes throughout the land. I will perpetuate your memory though all generations; therefore the nations will praise you for ever and ever.

Psalm 45:16-17 NIV

Table of Contents

Foreword

I watched the single life of Josh Seibert, then observed the courtship of Josh and Erika, and then heard from afar about the decline and final passing of this dear brother into glory. Now I am watching up close the "life after" of Erika. There are two ways I can identify with the people in this book. First, I am half of a ministry couple that is engaged with people's blessings and trials, just like she and Josh were for their brief but intensive four years together. Second, I also lost an immediate family member, just like Erika. For Helen and me, it was an immediate and unexpected loss, while Erika's loss involved a long and drawn out period of suffering. The differences in our situations do not matter, since we both have experienced the abundant grace of God which has gotten us through it all.

Erika, I believe, wrote this book to help herself through this period of grief and recovery. It is not an easy read but it is a book that you will deeply appreciate both for its honesty and for its steadfast faith in the midst of the hardest trial a couple could ever face. As writing the book has helped her triumph through her grief, reading this book will help you face whatever life will throw at you. Erika Seibert has shown that there is "life after." You can now discover her path and make it your own.

Dr. William Varner

Chapter 1

A Life Submitted to Christ

The borrowed time allotted to Josh Seibert, also known as J.D. Seibert, began on November 26th, 1979. He was the younger of two siblings born to Don and Kim Seibert in Southern California. From infancy, everyone knew Josh for his sweet smile and charm with people. He was a relatively small boy but appeared strong and healthy up until his adulthood. Josh grew up not only learning to crawl and walk, but also earning his fins as an excellent swimmer and avid surfer. The family spent their summers at the beach. His parents were believers who sought to raise their children in the fear and admonition of the Lord, although not without challenges along the way. His mom also helped in the youth group. She says Josh was a well-behaved boy and seldom recalls having to spank him. He professed faith as a young child.

As a teenager, it became apparent to Josh that either his initial profession of faith wasn't genuine, or he needed to re-dedicate his life to Christ. He recalled two events in his life that drove his need for the gospel home. The first was what started as a playful game with other boys and BB guns. The same kind that Ralph's mom from *The Christmas Story* warned would shoot his eye out. Parental supervision was not in the picture. The BB gun war ended with one of his friends in the hospital after a severe injury caused by Josh. Tension between the families arose, and things were never the same. The need for Christ's forgiveness came to the surface.

The second event God used to show Josh's need for resolute faith was a summer camp where Josh thought it would be amusing to jump in the lake... naked. Some of the girls took pictures of his bare bottom. The youth pastor, one of Josh's heroes, got word of it and was disappointed. He almost had to be sent home from camp that year. The youth pastor had a serious talk with him about sending him home.

Josh identified coming to know the Lord in his youth group after hearing the implications of the gospel. He realized he was not truly living out the gospel he claimed. God opened his eyes to see ways he was not whole-heartily following Christ. Josh then desired to surrender every aspect of his life to Christ as his Lord. This time marked a turning point of repentance and genuine salvation.

After being saved, Josh started a Christian punk rock band with some talented friends. Their heart was for their young punk rock generation to come under submission of Christ. They called themselves, "Youth in Submission." They proclaimed the gospel to other youth through music. They played at numerous venues in Los Angles and recorded two records, which came on ancient devices called cassettes or "tapes". Although most of the "music" sounded like screaming, Josh assured me that their fans read the words of the songs and sang along. Even then, he was a young evangelist. The following lyrics are from two songs that demonstrate the message he and his band sought to convey to their peers.

Youth in Submission

Preaching the word, you can hear it
Youth in submission, Youth in submission
Guided and directed by the Holy Spirit
Claiming the cross of Christ name
So turn to Him and get things right

Christ is the only way to life

So turn to Him and join the fight

Running the race set before us

Living the lives that He gave us

Taking a stand against the lies

Dead to the world, but alive to Christ

Youth in Submission, Youth in Submission (x4)

Focused

I don't want what the world offers

Cause only God's love will endure

Worldly things will fade away

But only God's love is here to stay

Satan's lies and deception

Will not steal away my redemption

I keep my eyes Focused on God

And I hate Satan's fraud

So much tries to sidetrack me

But through hard times I am free

I find hope in Jesus Christ

As I press forward for the prize

That I pursue to His utmost call

For Jesus Christ the savior of all

There's so many distractions and so many lies

But I will never compromise

Cause Christ is the only thing that's true

And His salvation for me and you

Worldly Things will all come to pass

But only God's will lasts

Josh attended a local public school called Canyon High. There he confronted the world on a daily basis. He told me of the struggles he faced and his resolve to live differently. For example, Josh's favorite hobby was skateboarding. He learned to do all kinds of tricks and spent many hours perfecting them. The skating scene included teens that smoked and did drugs. One day Josh got stopped by police as he was skating home. The officer abruptly pulled his cop car over to the side of the road to interrogate him. He shouted, "Where are you off to young man?" Josh calmly replied, "I'm on my way home sir." Dissatisfied the officer retorted, "You are going to smoke pot, aren't you?" Josh was taken aback and just shook his head in denial. The cop pulled him aside and searched his pants pockets. The officer was frustrated not to find any contraband on him. The only thing Josh had in his pocket was some lint and a Gideon's New Testament Bible. The cop was dumbfounded and let him go. The only contraband this youth possessed was the spiritual sword of the Word of God.

Josh had a heart for the lost youth. In college, he served as a youth pastor at a cowboy church where he learned the ropes as a cowboy, ministry, and Christ-like character. Josh was the kind of person that could do anything he set his mind to do. When he wanted to learn a new skill, he did not give up until he mastered it. If he felt God was calling him to a new venture, he thoroughly pursued it. Josh got to serve in many ways at the cowboy church. He taught Sunday school class, chaperoned camps, assisted in holding events, and helped in the yearly Easter play.

Josh also played the lead role of Jesus twice in an Easter sunrise play at Vasquez Rocks. One of those years Josh ended up getting very sick with pneumonia. He had a choice to back out of the performance after weeks of rehearsal and preparation or pull through and continue in the play. He chose to rough it out. To play the part of Jesus, he had to wear nothing but a thin white garment covering his groin. The weather was unusually cold that year. He had to stay out in the cold exposed for hours at a time for both the rehearsals and the two shows. One was in the evening and one in the early hours before the sun came out. Josh made it through the end of the last performance. Once he was done, they rushed him to the emergency room. Josh later expressed how impactful that event was in his life. He said the pain and anguish of the cross became so vivid to him—he identified with the pain Jesus felt on our behalf as He stood on the cross to replay its message to the audience. It was a life-changing experience for him—one that he would later re-live again, only within the wall of a hospital room in a different kind of sacrificial suffering.

There was much invaluable experience for Josh at the cowboy church. He got to live the cowboy scene at the ranch. They taught him how to rope, ride, brand and herd cattle. One particular horse that Josh invested much time into was called Mocha. I found a small title deed to Mocha in Josh's old files. In jest Josh bought Mocha for a dollar in exchange for working with her. Mocha was Josh's first horse, and both of them needed to be broken in.

Josh had to learn some things painfully. There was one incident where he dislocated his elbow from an accident with her. He was getting off of Mocha and accidentally pulled his leg over her head and startled her, causing her to jump and throw him off by his bare arm. Being in the outskirts of the city, it seemed like an eternity to Josh till his mom came and took him to the nearest hospital. His arm was never the same after that incident. He had earned his scars as a cowboy in training.

Josh participated in round-ups and worked at the ranch. He spent so much time there that he soon became like family. Besides working closely at the ranch, he also traveled often to other ranches to herd cattle including some cowboy clinics in Nevada and Montana. During this time, Josh composed cowboy poetry songs. He then recited his poems from memory. Three of his cowboy poems were featured on Western Horseman calendars. Josh recorded three professional albums with sound effects titled: *Bend or Break (2005), Rangeland Rhymes and Prairie Poems (2006)*, and *J.D. Seibert Cowboy Poetry (2008)*.

Josh thoroughly enjoyed composing poetry that told of the allures of the cowboy life. He memorized his poems and acted them out on stage at cowboy churches and cowboy festivals. Since Josh loved history, he joyfully took to performing for children and taught them through hands-on training. He showed the kids roping using a cow dummy. He was always thrilled to be invited to play, whether at a local school, large cowboy poetry festivals, or plain hay and barn church gatherings. Most notable was his love to share Christ with whatever microphone God placed in front of him. Cowboy poetry was another one of those mediums to proclaim the saving work of Christ in his life. The following poem captures the essence of Josh's heart.

Captured

Can Christ capture the heart of a cowboy?

Whose spirit roams wild and free

Pard, I dare say that it's true that he can

Because he captured the likes of me

Oh, how my wicked ways were woolly

And as wild as a savages cry

And if ere one could brag 'bout exploits

Surely it was I

For I'd lived upon the forsaken range
Not within earshot of demand
But it was my heart and not my ears
That heard the whisper of His command

He had tossed a well-placed loop
That I could not possibly evade
But now that he has captured me
I understand why I was made

It weren't merely for punchin' cattle
Despite all the boss's claims
And now I can be found in that book of life
Along with all them other names

For I've been branded with a new iron
That won't warsh off in the rain
And baptized in the redeeming blood
Of the precious lamb that was slain

And now as I reflect upon my life
And the shortcomings of my behavior
I can conclude of but one thing
I'm a great sinner, and He's a great Savior

Copyright Josh "J.D." Seibert 2010

Josh had quite the sense of humor and genuinely love people. He loved to make people laugh and entertain others. He would cross both cultural and ethnic barriers with his charm and humor. Josh took to composing and reciting poetry naturally. He started writing poetry in a personal journal during his adolescent years. Journaling translated into songwriting while leading the punk rock band, Youth in Submission. Later he continued to keep a journal of personal poems and reflections. As Josh grew more and more interested in the study of God's Word and ministry, his poems naturally grew meatier with more spiritual sustenance.

Josh used his various skills and talents as opportunities to proclaim the gospel. Throughout his young adult life, friends and family encouraged him to become a youth pastor. He continued to feel a pull towards ministry but wondered if that was his true calling. In college, he became interested in teaching high-school history and his desire to reach the youth for the gospel continued to grow. After receiving his teaching credential, he began teaching history in the public school system. Josh found it increasingly difficult to share the good news of Jesus in an environment that was hostile from teachers and students alike. The youth at his school were interested only in devising wickedness. They bullied and ridiculed others, including Josh, and deviously locked Josh in the bathroom one afternoon. They had no respect for their parents or anyone else in authority. He found that civics could never address the student's need for the life-giving words of the gospel.

Josh's call to preach the gospel became most apparent when it came time for him to teach his students about the Declaration of Independence. When it came time to tell the students about who created all men equal, the public school system asked him to remain silent. He felt as if his hands were tied. Upon going through the founding documents of America, he couldn't help but want to declare not only who their founding fathers were, but who the heavenly Father was. He didn't want to talk to his students about the rights and privileges afforded to them as American citizens, but about the greater rights and privileges they had if they became citizens of heaven. Speaking of the blood that was shed by men to purchase momentary freedom was not as precious to him as telling them about the bloodshed by one man for their eternal freedom from sin. Josh found himself not wanting to teach the punk rockers, goths, jocks, skater dudes, surfers and cheerleaders that their problems were results of poverty, inequality or unequal distribution of wealth or lack of education but that their real problem was sin and their rebellion against God. He grew tired of teaching the kids that government, politicians, or politics would save them and desired to impress on them that the only salvation possible was through Christ alone. It was then, after two years of teaching American history that Josh felt a desire to pursue full-time ministry.

Josh enrolled at The Master's Seminary (TMS) with the encouragement of his pastors. He spent half of the last decade of his life studying. It was the prominent place to study as Josh grew up in Santa Clarita Valley where Pastor John MacArthur's ministry permeated. In seminary, he served in the youth group staff at his home church where he could apply what he learned in school. God used this time in his life to give him practical ministry experience, and training in exegesis and theology that could come aside to bolster his teaching. However, he could not imagine how short a time for ministry God allotted.

At TMS, Josh also got to visit Israel and enjoyed a tour with one of the Old Testament professors, Dr. Varner. It was inspiring for him to visit historical biblical sites. He said it made the Bible come alive in a way he hadn't experienced. He also went on several short-term missions trips with his church. Most notably in his mind, however, was the life lesson of learning not to be stingy with his limited time while in school. Josh devoted himself to service for the Lord. He found that when he didn't selfishly use his time for his academic accomplishment, God would multiply it. When he was generous with his time in ministry, he still seemed to have ample time for his other responsibilities.

It was not easy all the time to juggle work, ministry, and seminary. Josh grew discouraged from time to time. He felt unworthy and like a lousy speaker. He told the story of a professor who compared him to Woody Allen in preaching class. Josh said most seminary students only had to take one preaching lab class, but he had to take two. The Lord used these classes and his experience teaching the youth to grow his speaking ability and confidence as a spokesman of God rather than relying on himself. From time to time he was tempted toward insecurity, and then went back to where his courage for preaching came from—the authority of God's Word and his training to divide it accurately.

Seminary equipped Josh with everything he needed to prepare for ministry. However, there was one thing missing. He was single and was afraid of being in the small percentage of those who came in single and left alone. He had been praying for a helpmate for ministry. He dated several girls while in seminary. None seemed to work in God's providences. Then, Josh met a girl whose prayer caught his attention. The lucky girl was me. However, there was one problem. I was dating his friend. He then began praying for me to be his. During Josh's last semester at the seminary in spring of 2013, he chose to redeem me as his bride.

I was a relatively new Christian and a single unwed mother with Noah. My parents brought me up in a Catholic home with good morals. We were traditionally religious, especially during calamity such as the death of a loved one or disasters like the 1994 Northridge earthquake. What was missing was a personal saving relationship with Jesus. My prayers were selfish and superficial. A deeply seeded rebellion simmered in my heart. It was manifested in disobedience to my parents, breaking the rules and getting suspended from high school. It was my quest for love in all the wrong places that continually left me in shambles. I eventually got pregnant out of wedlock and almost had an abortion. Thanks to a crisis pregnancy center, Noah was born. It took rejection from Noah's father, heartbreak and abuse for me to realize the wreckage of my sin and need to turn to Christ for salvation. It was during a crusade event that the Holy Spirit opened my eyes to the glory of the gospel that God sent His perfect, holy Son to die to take His just wrath for all my sins. The evangelist had just lost his son, yet had genuine peace knowing his son was in heaven, not based on being a "good" person, but because of his son's faith in Christ as Savior.

That day, I committed to following Christ and abstained from my former immoral lifestyle. I was still alone and a single mom naïve on how to biblically raise my child. I had been praying for a family God's way and marriage since August of 2008 when God saved me. God used those four and a half years of waiting to grow my dependence on my heavenly Redeemer and Father. Then, he graciously gave me away to my beloved husband. Josh was my earthly kinsman redeemer. He took me as I was and did not merely see my dark past, but the beauty of redemption. The way Josh graciously saw it, we were both saving each other from singleness. Josh exemplified the selfless love of God's adoption of us as his children by being eager to take on Noah as his own. In many ways, our marriage was a picture of the gospel of Jesus dying to win and purify an unworthy bride to God's glory. Josh died to himself in many ways when he took Noah and me under his wings.

This memoir book tells our story. It is a story of redemption, romance, drama, suffering, and glory. Our story is only part of a grand novel of the greatest love of all time—the love of Christ for His bride. My prayer is that our story would display Christ and His abundant love and care for His own.

Josh's life taught many. He touched all that knew him, and even those who never personally knew him, but were inspired by his unshakable joy and faithfulness to the gospel. His example continues to influence others. Throughout his life, Josh kept his focus on winning others to Christ till his dying breath. He would pray for others and seek to minister even when his body was worn and weak. His passion never ceased telling of the great story of Jesus and His love. This memoir celebrates the life of a real man of God whose unwavering faith and his walk with Christ will live on far beyond the short life that he was granted here on this earth.

Where Moth and Rust Destroy

Those moths sure seem determined

To do a number on my sleeve

And I reckon that not even mothballs

Will encourage them to leave

I picked this Pendleton up last week

I ain't even had it fer very long

Guess the lure of nicely nit wool

To a moth is mighty strong

Seems like everyone's days are numbered

With conception and a prime

And long before its days are over

It's gone before its time

I've got a pair of Ol' Garcia spurs

With rowels of sixteen points

But so much rust has taken to em

That they're frozen at the joints

The rowels just froze there in their place

They no longer will spin free

And though they're of sentimental value

They ain't much good to me

But I keep em around anyway

They make good bookends or paperweights

But they'll never return to their former glory

Or regain their early traits

And such seems the very nature

Of the many things I own

And I ain't been able to store or keep

Much of the treasure that I've known

I even got my favorite saddle stole

Without hope of gettin it back

Now, I don't mind partin with other things

But never steal a cowboy's tack

And things not of eternal value

Or intrinsic in their worth

Just don't seem to last too long

During their days upon the earth

So I'll store up treasure fer myself

In a place that's true and real

Where moth and rust do not destroy

Or thieves break in and steal

[Chapter 2]

We Didn't Call It Love at First Sight

J osh and I met at the Ronald Reagan Library spring of 2010. We were on a date, yet not with each other. I was on a date with one of his friends from seminary, and he was there with another girl. The four of us were waiting in line to walk through Air Force One. We all started chatting and getting to know one another. My date and Josh were good seminary buddies. A friend of mine had set me up with a man who asked her for a blind date with the godliest woman she knew; my sweet friend somehow thought I fit the description. After our blind date, the seminarian started pursing me for marriage. He felt called to serve as a missionary in Cameroon, and my heart was fond of mission work. One of my spiritual gifts is evangelism, so I thought this was the call of my life too. We dated for about eight months.

As we continued to date, I accompanied him to a Bible study he led that Josh attended. I don't remember much of Josh back then. I only had eyes for "my man." The only faint memory I have is of one conversation where Josh and I agreed on grading in the educational system, and my boyfriend at the time didn't agree with our viewpoint. I didn't think much of it. My first impression of Josh was simply that he was a nice guy. I had no idea we would end up married; I thought I would marry his friend. Josh, on the other hand, said he liked me from the start. He later revealed, "Erika what attracted me to you was the way you prayed." From that point on, Josh prayed that his friend and I would break up. Ironically, it was according to God's will, because we later broke up.

I was heartbroken after our break-up and would not have been happy to hear of Josh's prayer. In my world of being a single mother, it was a trial to date with intentions of marriage only to break up nearly a year later. Looking back at it, I see the hand of God in teaching me how the heartaches of life can be the biggest blessings. The Lord grew my trust and dependence on Him through my broken dreams and prepared me for an even deeper wound in years to come. Moreover, had it not been for dating him, I may not have met and married Josh.

Several months after the break-up, Josh and I saw each other on campus at Grace Community Church. He attended The Master's Seminary while I worked at Grace Community School as a teacher's assistant. I have endearing memories of him starting conversations with me. We crossed paths often. It was providential that we would end up at the same place at the same time. A couple of those conversations ended with him asking me out for lunch.

The first time he asked me out I was already dating someone else. My spiritual mentor set me up with a widower. I told Josh this, but he insisted in asking me out two more times. All the while things with the widower didn't seem to be going anywhere. I was willing to give it some time since he had tragically lost his wife and was left with four children to raise on his own. My mentor suggested I give him three months to make a decision about me, so I did. We both had children, so it complicated things and further made it necessary to cut our dating time short to guard the children's hearts. When three months had passed the widower wanted to remain friends.

Around the same time, Josh and I saw each other at an ice skating fundraiser for a mission's trip hosted by the singles ministry he attended. That night Josh followed us around the arena. I hoped Josh would keep pursuing me after that. However, he had given up. Years later, when re-telling our story, he said, "I had the three strikes, and you're out policy in asking girls out." I had struck out. We had corresponded about a book on prayer by John MacArthur called *At the Throne of Grace*. I sent him a message asking if he'd like me to mail him the book. He warmly invited me to bring Noah to an annual Vacation Bible School (VBS) children's program his church was hosting. I almost didn't take Noah because he was already attending VBS that week in the mornings and it was out of the way. Since it was a long drive, I ended up staying at the church while Noah attended VBS.

That night, Josh shared several of his poems and short stories with me. He then asked if we could go on a hike the next day before the start of VBS. I said yes, and we took Noah with us on a trail at Placerita Canyon Nature Center. We enjoyed the hike. Josh made Noah laugh with his funny knock-knock jokes. There was much smiling and laughing. Josh set a happy mood by making our hike light-heartened. I was impressed by his tenderness, and a kindred love for children. He was tender with Noah even when my young boy would disobey. Even though Josh was interested in me, he was attentive to Noah just as much as to me. He showed genuine Christ-like love.

Later I learned Josh considered our hike our first date. For me going anywhere with my son did not feel like a date. He then asked me out for lunch and started calling me. Every day Josh texted me to say he was praying for my day. This felt more like the beginning of a new relationship. Our friendship turned into a relationship officially on Facebook when I changed my status. His comment was, "The cat is out of the bag!" This was the same year that Facebook had gone public. By then it was already a major form of communication for all our friends and even family. Most of our friends found out we were dating on social media. It had just become the new medium for finding out the latest news.

Josh and I dated for four months. He took us out to restaurants, hikes, mini-golf, museums, and movies. One of our first dates was a fun 50s dance social his church put together. At the social, Josh introduced me to his friends, and we all danced in a circle. We also went on a double-date with his friend that I had dated prior to Josh. It was a bit awkward for me. It was the first time I chose to submit to him on something I didn't necessarily agree on. We all went to out for coffee and Frisbee golf and ended up having a wonderful time.

One of the things I loved about Josh the most was how much he made me laugh. He knew how to enjoy life. Every time we went out we had such a good time. Whether it was in a group setting or just the two of us, there was never a dull moment. On one occasion, I remember us going to a special showing of the first Hobbit movie. They were serving a second breakfast of pancakes and sausage before the film. There were many people we didn't know, but we quickly made new friends. Josh was amiable and made friends wherever we went.

Josh connected with people quickly. This held especially true with Noah. He not only won my heart but his as well. Josh would not neglect to take Noah on some of our dates. We took him with us to museums such as the Skirball Cultural Center, the Getty Center and the Word Ink and Blood Exhibit where we saw fragments of the Dead Sea Scrolls. It was harder for Noah to be a behaved boy at these places that required him to keep quiet and not touch anything. Despite Noah's restlessness and full-throttle energy, Josh patiently and lovingly welcomed him into his busy life.

Josh also invited us to tag along with him to the many youth group events he organized. This helped us get to know each other in natural settings. At the same time, he was careful to guard our hearts and our purity. He decided it would be wise for Noah and me to keep attending our home church until we were engaged. The plan was that if we were to get engaged, then I would switch churches to attend the church where Josh worked as a youth pastor.

As our relationship progressed, we often had meals with his parents or mine. Josh's parents started praying early on. They were kind and supportive of our relationship. My parents enjoyed Josh's sense of humor as he often made up jokes in Spanish. They appreciated his attempt at speaking Spanish and his taste for Mexican food. Josh had asked my dad for his permission to date me. The notion of asking for permission to date his 27-year old daughter was peculiar to my dad, but he was appreciative. The last guy who had asked if he could date me said he'd take me to Africa if we married, so my dad was much more inclined.

Josh was busy in seminary, so there were times our date consisted of me quizzing him on his flashcards. I would cook dinner, and then ask him questions about key Bible passages after our meal. Josh would move my small round glass kitchen table and set it outside in front of my apartment door, which worked since my little one-bedroom apartment was downstairs. We probably looked strange eating and hanging out in front of our entire neighborhood, but nobody seemed to mind. Staying outside kept us accountable with our church friends who were also my neighbors and would check on us from their living room window. We were just so glad to be able to have meals together and spend time together. After dinner, we would go out for walks. I lived two miles from Castaic Lake, which made walking to the lake a regular and inexpensive activity. A few times we saw a couple coyotes from a distance. I felt safe when Josh was with us. He also wanted to teach Noah how to fish at the lake. That's when we both knew we wanted to do life together.

The more we dated, the more we realized how perfect we were for each other. We both had a heart for ministry. We had the same convictions. Many of our preferences were the same too. We both loved the same kind of food. Even though I am Mexican-American and Josh was Caucasian, he ate spicier food than me. Most notably we both had the passion for sharing the gospel with others. On several occasions we shared the good news of salvation together. One warm day, we went to the beach in Santa Monica to do evangelism together. We got to share with a woman selling handmade merchandise on the walkway. She had many questions. Josh was thankful to allow another woman to talk to her and he mostly prayed while I spoke. He then shared with a young man that looked high but was eager to accept Christ if he could keep his mistress of Mary Jane (marijuana) as well. Josh explained how one must be willing to leave all behind and forsake sin to follow Jesus. While he shared, I prayed. It would have been dangerous for me to go to this area of Santa Monica by myself. Together we were a great team!

This dating time was exciting, yet it also made me nervous. I was afraid if it didn't work out, Noah's high hopes of having a dad would be dashed. I told Josh of my previous three-month rule and was determined to stick with it. Around month three, he started talking about getting me a ring, and soon after took me shopping to pick one out. For me it wasn't about the ring; what was most important was his character and love for the Lord. The price of the ring didn't matter, especially since he couldn't afford much as a seminary student and part-time youth pastor. We found a beautiful white gold ring with a small diamond and sparkly jewels around it in the shape of a swirl. I knew he was going to propose, but I didn't know when, where or how. I was content to know Josh was the one. It was one of the most thrilling seasons of my life. I could hardly take the suspense. Noah was just as excited too.

Our coming together was more challenging to navigate than the average couple since we had a blended family. We had to be sensitive to Noah. God was kind to allow this transition to be as smooth as it could have possibly been. Noah wanted to have a dad in his life. He was genuinely happy for us and didn't express any fear or anxiety. Josh was solely marrying me, but he was also taking on my son as his own. Pastor Michael Mahoney was one of the Spanish pastors and agreed to marry us in a bilingual gospel-centered ceremony. We came to know Pastor Mahoney better during our pre-marital counseling. He shared his personal testimony of how perfect God had matched not only him and his wife, but also a son they adopted. This was true of Josh and Noah too. Noah was full of energy and always wanted to explore new places and do things outdoors. Josh likewise was playful and always on the hunt for an adventure. He loved to plan trips and take us to new places to do things we had never tried. Josh was eager to teach Noah different things like how to throw a baseball or surf.

On Josh's 33rd birthday, he planned a trip to Carpentaria State beach. We drove with Josh's parents and Noah. We enjoyed swimming in the ocean and playing in the sand. Josh taught Noah how to catch some waves. His mom and dad watched Noah while Josh took me on a walk along the bluffs. I suspected an upcoming proposal. Yet, I had been expecting it for a few weeks and was prepared to wait longer. Then, the moment we had been anticipating—he got down on one knee and asked me to marry him. He had the ring in one hand and a card in the other. He knew how much I loved to scrapbook and make cards. So he had sneaked into a ladies card-making event at the church to make me two beautiful cards. He gave me the first as a foretaste of the proposal that would soon follow. The cards read:

November 16, 2012

My Dearest Love Erika,

The Lord is so good in providing me with such a great friend and love in you and I am so thankful for you and all that the Lord is doing in our relationships. I am so excited to move forward with you as we progress to marriage and can't wait to spend the rest of my life with you as your husband! I love you so much and want to give you all the love that I have. Know that I pray for you daily and I am seeking God's guidance and blessing for us!

Love

Josh Seibert

Proposal card:

November 24, 2012

My Dearest Love in all the World

Today is the very day you and I have been waiting for... when I ask you to be my wife for this life. I am so excited for what God is doing in our lives, and I can't wait to begin our lives together as we become one flesh in body and spirit in marriage. I vow to be a good, God-fearing, husband to you and a father to Noah; and I will make it my life's endeavor to serve and lay down my life for you as Christ did the church.

Love, your fiancé,

Josh Seibert

Josh was hoping I'd say yes, and I did. It was one of our most delightful days together. It made for an unforgettable birthday for him. He had been praying for the gift of a wife for most of his life. There was a sense of peace and comfort from the Lord, the day we could call each other fiancé. It was staggering to think of God's kindness to provide a wonderful soul mate with whom we thought we'd spend the rest of our lives together. Though the length of our marriage was shorter than expected, in the mind and plan of God, the number of days we would share as one flesh was set. Our engagement went pretty fast. We couldn't wait to be wed and desired to honor God and remain pure.

Valentine's Day was a special day for me. The Lord saved me as a single mom out of an immoral lifestyle on August 16, 2008. By God's grace, the Spirit worked a powerful and transforming work of repentance in my life. Soon after, I started praying for a godly husband and father for Noah. February 14, 2009, was my first Valentine's Day as a born-again Christian. I had just turned 25. I was sad God hadn't answered my prayer for a date that day. Noah was only two years old so I decided to take him on the trolley. He had been wanting to go on the 'train' for some time.

That date with little Noah, my heart was flooded with God's love. The Lord used a verse reference printed on the bottom of a Forever 21 shopping bag to open the door for me to share the gospel with a young girl. It was exhilarating. I remember driving to the train station and asking God to reveal to me the extent of His love. On our way home, I was awestruck by the thought of how overwhelmingly great His love is. I told Josh this story, and we agreed on a Valentine's Day wedding. Josh was happy our anniversary would be easier to remember. I thought it sweet of the Lord to answer my prayer for a "date" on Valentine's Day four years later with a husband.

Our colors were bright pink and white. It went perfectly with our Valentine's Day theme. At first, I hesitated to use the shade of pink as it was such a girly color. I mentioned to Josh other colors like purple or melon. Then, I shared how one of my cousins chose fuchsia for her wedding. Josh said he liked the pink I picked, and that was the end of the discussion. I was eager to come under his authority and he just couldn't wait to make me his bride.

My mother-in-law and some friends hosted beautiful bridal parties. Josh's niece, made the best paper bouquet. For one of the games, I had to guess how Josh answered some questions. I was surprised at how many I got wrong. That is when I learned that he considered our hike with Noah our first date. There were many other things I thought I knew about Josh that I really had no idea. Dating was in some respects like a dream come true. Half the time I was on cloud nine with sweet butterflies and fanciful dreams of our life together. It was a pure kind of love in which it was so easy to believe the best in each other. It was bliss. We were ready to take our relationship to a new level—one that would be more centered on reality.

About the same time as our engagement many people were afraid of the world coming to an end. There was a group of supposed religious people that believed December 21, 2012, would mark the end of the world. Josh and I were not concerned. We believed Matthew 13 that said, "But concerning that day or that hour, no one knows, not even the angels in heaven, nor the Son, but only the Father." That fact alone meant that it was not likely the December date predicted. Moreover, we knew that with our faith rooted in Christ alone for salvation we were ready to face whatever may come in the future.

Preparations for our wedding soon came to full swing as we had only three months to plan the entire thing. All our close friends pitched in to help. It was amazing to see the church come together to make our wedding not only possible, but also unforgettable. We didn't have much money. I had been a part-time tutor and single mom, while Josh was a youth intern and a seminary student. Still, God provided for all of it through the church, family, and friends. The church hosted our wedding at no cost. Josh's dad paid for our photography. My dad covered dinner, one of my sisters took care of the cake, and another provided for my accessories. We had friends give us wedding gifts like flower arrangements, cupcakes, a wedding video, hair and makeup, and party planning. The only things I paid for were my wedding dress and the decorations. Pinterest helped me with inexpensive decorations that were cute and added a personal touch. Two girls from the youth group helped make the pinwheels for the table centerpieces. On top of all of these amazing arrangements, Josh's grandmother Gigi gave him his grandfather's gold wedding band. It was astounding to see how God provided for everything from the small details for our wedding to the big provisions that meant the world to us.

Our wedding day was beautiful. We were married February 15, 2013, at the sweet church where Josh served as youth pastor. My father, Servando, walked me down the aisle with joy. Josh was the most delighted groom. My heart was full of anticipation and praise to God for answering years of earnest prayers for a kinsman redeemer. Pastor Mahoney performed a simple, yet theologically rich ceremony in English and Spanish.

Just as we did during Josh's proposal, we had a ceramic bowl of water with a towel to wash each other's feet. This was a symbol of how we vowed to humbly serve one another in marriage. It would characterize the way he would care for me when I was sick, and how I cared for him while he was dying, "The act of foot washing pointed to the greatest act of humility and service in the history of the world. There in the upper room we have a glimpse of what Jesus did on the cross. The disciples were expecting military messiah, and instead they had a suffering servant who would humbly lay down his life in weakness and shame to cleanse his people's sin" (*Furman*, 73)

Foot washing was Josh's idea, and he had other creative plans for the wedding, but not all of them were feasible. One was to have a box with sand. He wanted to draw the ictus sign with his finger in the sand, and have me complete it with mine. Logistically this would have been hard to pull off. I appreciated his heart to exalt Christ from the commencement of our marriage, and his involvement in planning our ceremony

Following the official wedding ceremony, we went into the church offices to sign the legal documents. After we signed the paperwork upstairs, Josh and I went into his office to have a glass of sparkling cider and a personal toast to each other. All the while, our wonderful church and our sweet friends were turning the church into a reception banquet, and our guests had appetizers out front. Noah and the kids had a piñata to break during this short interlude. The program was genius and planned by Josh with the help of the church staff. It was a small church so we could only invite 200 guests to our wedding. This meant our guests were mostly our large family and a few close friends. My best friend traveled from Minnesota to be the matron of honor, and Noah got to be the ring bearer. Josh's brother-in-law, nephew, and another close friend put on a funny bandito skit where they robbed our guests for honeymoon money.

Our two honeymoons were also gifts from the Lord through the generosity of others. Since Josh had papers due and exams right after our wedding, we stayed only the weekend at a bed and breakfast in Three Rivers that a gracious couple hosts for seminary student and their wives to stay. Then during his Spring Break, we went on a more extended honeymoon. Through the seminary, Josh found another generous couple that let us stay in their guest house in Malibu. We were thrilled to get to enjoy two fun honeymoons. We called them our short and long honeymoon. We would continue to see the Lord's provision for our family throughout our married life and even after Josh's home-going. During our wedding, we had a guest book where our friends and loved ones could write a note of encouragement. Josh decided we should use this journal to write letters to one other throughout our marriage and chronicle our journey together.

February 15, 2013

Good day My Love, or should I say the best day of my life? It is today, the day of our wedding that we will begin to live our lives together as husband and wife! Words cannot express how grateful and thankful to God I am for you. You are truly the love of my life, and God has made you such a wonderful suited helpmate for me! As I put our slideshow together for the wedding, I was just struck by all of the good times and blessings that we've enjoyed together. I am looking forward to a whole lifetime of more. I am also so looking forward to spending time with you on our honeymoon and showing you Sequoia National Park!

Love, your soon to be… in six hours, husband,

Josh

February 23, 2013

My dearest love and joy,

You are the best gift I could ever dream of! Being your wife is all I've wanted and more! The honeymoon was amazing… it is an experience that I never want to forget! The emotions I felt were a bit overwhelming; yet filled my heart with so much joy and awe at what God has done in bringing us together as one! Your love is deep and unconditional—much like Christ's love for the church. I'm so happy to get to serve you all the days of my life and to come under your provision and wise leadership. I anticipate growing old and sanctified together as we seek to fulfill God's will and honor Him. I love that you have us read things like Songs of Solomon or the Love and Respect book! Thank you sweetie!

Love, tu esposa (your wife)

The Great Trinitarian Romance

God is a great Romancer

One Who loves to love

A divine courtship takes place

[35]

In His heavenly courts above

For it is He Who courts Himself
With all the affection of a suitor
Like a beau, He woos His beloved
For He is love's greatest tutor

The writings of Byron, Shelly, and Keats
Pose as no competition
For the Romantic musings of God
In the Bible's composition

For the Father loves the Son
And the Son Himself is sent
The Holy Spirit then testifies
Of a love that won't relent

From these Lovers, we take our lead
Modeling the blessed Godhead
Who exemplify the standard
For how mere mortals are to wed

[Chapter 3]

M&Ms: Marriage & Ministry

M arriage proved to be delightfully sweet. It is one of the greatest gifts given by God to mankind. Our first few weeks together were some of the best days of our lives. We were newlyweds and filled with so much excitement and joy. It felt so rewarding to cook and clean with a man in the house. Tending to my home became less of a chore and more of a labor of love. I made sure to pack Josh the most delicious lunch I could muster, and kept our home tidy. One of Josh's favorite things was having me pack him a lunch with a romantic note in it. He told me he bragged to his seminary friends about it. Cooking for a family, and specifically for a man inspired me to be a better cook. My six-year-old son, Noah, had previously generally been content with hot dogs and macaroni. Meals used to be simple. Now, there was an expectation of at least one full hearty meal that would fill a grown man's stomach. I desired to please my husband so I made meals he relished. In time, this presented itself as an added challenge, mainly because I was not a seasoned cook and he could be a picky eater. Parenting was so much more natural for me with a male authority figure in our home. Josh taking Noah in as an adoptive parent posed its unique challenges. However, during the first couple of months, even the problems were gladly welcomed.

The "honeymoon stage" was short-lived. We began our marriage with two blessings and challenges—children and ministry.

Josh was already a pastor when I married him. I was already a parent when he married me. When we came together, he got an instant family, and I became an instant pastor's wife. It took some time and adjustment from living single, but we managed. We had to learn to move away from our independence to depend on each other. We had to die to our preferences and grow in selflessness.

Besides the struggles from within, the world around us also changed right before our eyes. It had become increasingly more and more uncertain since 911. Precisely two months after our wedding, we heard of the atrocities of the Boston Marathon shooting. Our hearts broke for the families that lost loved ones. Everyone was gripped with terror. Some speculated that the government incited the events to spark fear that would give way to more governmental control and laws that would unarm citizens.

On top of the changes going on in the world, our family experienced changes of our own. Precisely 15 months into being married Josh went from being single to having a family of three with one new baby boy and one spiritually adopted eight-year-old son. All this family life happened simultaneously while serving in ministry.

The day I married Josh, I became a pastor's wife, and Noah became a pastor's kid. Josh had been serving as a youth pastor at Church of the Canyons. I began attending with him as soon as we got engaged. In fact, Josh had planned a winter camp the week before our wedding, and I gladly went with him. We decided I would serve alongside Josh in youth ministry as a female leader. The first significant parenting decision we had to make was if we'd allow Noah to come with us to youth group. We decided yes and then had to revise that decision when some parents didn't agree. This would be another of those early lessons on submission. In this case, it was not only an issue of me submitting to my husband but of both of us submitting to the church leadership, who also happened to be his boss. One of the parents graciously paid a babysitter for us. That helped settle the issue.

Noah loved Josh and was so happy to have a father in the home. At the same time, he soon found that having a dad meant an additional person parenting him. Noah tested his added authority. Josh did a great job at immediately stepping in and functioning as Noah's dad. It was amazing to see the almost immediate positive difference it made for Noah. Before I married, Noah was late for school practically every day. Josh made a big difference by merely helping get us out the door in the mornings. Noah's grades improved in school, and so did his behavior. He actually received an award at school for being the most improved student. Noah never saw Josh as anything less than a father. In fact, he wanted to call Josh dad even before we were married. From the day we said "I do", Noah gained a daddy in Josh and called him by this most endearing term of affection. He called him Daddy, Dad, and even Pop at times. Noah never called him step-dad. There was tension from Noah's biological father, because he wanted Noah to refer to Josh as step-dad. Noah relayed to us how he had been so upset that he told his biological father that he was his stepdad. Noah didn't fully understand the terminology. Josh married me and made it clear to Noah that he was now his own son. Our home was filled with his presence every day. He was there during dinner time and when it was time to tuck him in at night. Josh showed Noah the purest love of a father—love from above gained from the love that our heavenly Father had shown Josh.

Our new little family enjoyed living in Southern California and serving at Church of the Canyons. However, Josh wanted to provide for me to be able to stay at home. He began to look for a full-time job. Since we didn't know how long it would take for God to open a full-time pastoral position, that summer we moved out of our one-bedroom apartment in Castaic and into a two-bedroom home in the middle of the Los Angeles forest about thirty minutes from town. It was a beautiful but secluded place where our rent was discounted in exchange for Josh feeding the horses. It took us three weeks to hook up a phone line—our cell service didn't work out there. At night we heard strange noises that kept us awake. Josh told me it was Sasquatch. He had a motto he taught Noah, "Scaring is caring, and staring is impolite." The noises sounded like a cross between an owl and a monkey. It was quite frightening, especially one night that Josh grew scared. He took his gun out to shoot the possible intruder. This made me even more terrified.

I was relieved when Josh answered a call from a small church of about 250-300 people in Kingman, Arizona. They were looking for a youth pastor, and Josh was given the opportunity to visit for the weekend to candidate for the position. The pastor and his wife kindly hosted us in their home, showed us around town, and gave us the scoop on the best places we could explore. The highlight was getting to visit the Grand Canyon. It was the first time for Noah and me. We also looked at two homes that a church member was ready to rent to us at unbelievable prices. That Sunday, they had a party at their house and invited some of the parents from the youth group. We were having a good time with everyone until I started choking while I was eating, laughing and trying to talk at the same time. One of the parents was a doctor and came to my rescue with the Heimlich maneuver. What a first impression that must have been!

The church was loving and gracious. By the following Sunday evening, the church had made a unanimous vote to call Josh to be the new youth pastor. We were excited to begin a new journey together. Josh was most enthusiastic. He fell in love with the people and was not deterred by the desert heat. I was a bit more apprehensive. Perhaps it was the fact that I almost choked to death that scared me.

Nevertheless, I trusted Josh's leadership and would have followed him wherever God led. I knew God would go with us and send saving help if we were to need it. The church helped us move and get settled right away. Josh started at College Park Baptist Church in August of 2013.

— ⋅ — ⋅ —

September 26, 2013

Well, we've been in Kingman about a month, and I am so thankful that you are living this new life with our family and me. God is teaching us so much about what it means to honor him and die to self. I am so thankful for your commitment to Him and me. You're also doing a great job with getting to know all the people at church and loving them. We are so blessed to be here! I am so thankful that God has given you to me as my helpmate, and you are doing such an excellent job as we continue to learn our roles. Now as we set out for Cali for a few days, I look forward to seeing our friends and family.

Love,

Hubs

This was a big move and a drastic change for all of us after only six months of being a new family. The Lord provided the needed grace. Our church in Kingman made the transition a fun adventure for Noah. Our pastor was a big Green Bay Packers fan and turned Noah into one as well. Early on, Noah had bought him a little Packers action figure that he hid in a new place each time he visited his office. Everyone welcomed and loved our family. I never felt like I had to cower in shame over my past. Youth ministry was more of a challenge than the previous church in that we had to start from scratch. However, we were immensely blessed with the strong support of parents, as well as a good starting base of committed students.

We missed our family and friends but visited them often. We were in the middle of the desert in rural Kingman. Our church family embraced us and taught us how to enjoy things like fishing and hunting. A sweet couple married for fifty years, Jerry and Belinda Cook, adopted our family and taught us things like how to squirrel hunt and shoot a bow and arrow. We had a small army of wonderful friends in the church to support us. They became our second family.

The parents were tremendously supportive when I became pregnant during our first year in ministry together. Our little family at home was being solidified. Josh and I had decided to wait to try for children until he had a steady full-time job. Shortly after moving to Kingman, I asked Josh if we could start trying for a baby. The day he said yes, we prayed together asking God to gift us with a child. A couple weeks later I found out I was pregnant! The miraculous thing was that unbeknownst to us at the time, people with his disease are not usually able to have kids of their own. We soon found out we were having a boy whom we named Nathan. It was the only name on which we could both agree. His name means gift of God—that is exactly what he was. The parents in our youth group welcomed our new addition to not only our family, but also to the youth group! Thanks to their encouragement, we brought the baby along. As he grew older, some of the moms took Nathan to another room to play. The church was beyond generous with the arrival of our baby. The moms from our youth group and the pastor's wife organized a huge cowboy themed, church-wide baby shower. I have never received so many gifts in my life. Nathan had more than everything he needed.

Josh had wanted to name him Shamgar from Judges 3:31 after the warrior who saved Israel by defeating 600 Philistines with an oxgoad. He felt it was a strong and warrior-type name. When I was pregnant, Josh called him Shamgar or Sammy in jest. Soon we found that more people would ridicule his name and decided to spare our child of the humiliation. However, we did keep it as a middle name. Josh said that the new generation needed more courageous men, so the title stuck.

We planned to have another child closely after Nathan so they could grow up together. However, God had another plan. I was diagnosed with a thyroid condition that made it necessary for me to take a strong medication harmful to the baby. If I ended up pregnant, there would be the possibility of putting the baby at risk or my own life during labor. I dreamed of having a little girl. In God's providence, we had no more children after that. When my thyroid issues resolved, we tried for another child with no success. Later Josh received a diagnosis for a disease he was born with that greatly decreases fertility. God's "no" made us more appreciative of His "yes" and the gift of Nathan's life.

Nathan was weaned at about a year old, and started having problems with his tummy. We didn't know the source of his discomfort. We took him to the doctor, who suggested we try a non-substitute dairy formula. That did the trick, and we learned he was allergic to dairy. He also had frequent ear infections, colic, and strep throat as a little guy. Nights were rough. Josh ended up sleeping on the couch nearly every night to not be constantly woken by the baby. It was a time God used for our sanctification as we endured sleepless nights.

Josh didn't do well with lack of sleep. Most of the time he was already functioning on low energy. We later found out he had been operating on low blood counts too. Josh wasn't worried about himself. He wanted to sleep so that he could do his ministry well and provide for our family. His biggest worry was for the health and well-being of his family. Little Nathan was tiny and fragile in his eyes. It was Josh's first baby, so he was extra cautious with him. Josh researched things that were toxic for babies and steered us away from them. He always made sure the baby had sunscreen when he went out in the sun. Josh even got little Nathan ear muffs for the periodic youth concerts we attended.

That year, the Ebola epidemic became a global health crisis. Even though the virus mostly affected Africa, the world was afraid of it spreading when two men traveled into the United States with the disease, died from it and infected a couple of nurses treating them. Josh was careful to wipe everything down when out in public, especially for the baby when at a restaurant or out grocery shopping. Josh encouraged me to stay away from public changing tables and preferred we change Nathan in the back of the car.

***

July 3, 2014

My dearest love Erika,

I am so proud of how you are allowing God to change and grow you more into the image of His Son. The girls at youth group really look up to you, and you are having a good impact on them! I am also thankful for all your hard work and commitment to breastfeeding 'Shammy' even though it takes many sleepless nights. Be encouraged to know that God is sanctifying us through the trials of marriage so that we can more accurately represent Him to the church and the world. As the old hymn goes, "The flame will not hurt you, I only design your dross to consume and your gold to refine." God has much gold in our marriage to refine. But when He is through it will be one beautiful treasure.

Love, Josh

Ministry was especially challenging. We went into complicated situations in need of being addressed biblically without an established framework or experience doing so. This took much time, prayer, and learning. There was a giant elephant in the room. Marriage was not being held in honor. Some in leadership argued for the church to accept unbiblical grounds for divorce. Josh had to take an unpopular stand against sin. Being caught up in the middle of it made us vulnerable in several ways. From within, some saw us as legalistic. We were tempted to anger in the flesh. Josh was able to maintain his composure and seek peace.

During this time, Josh decided to put hedges around our marriage. He realized that just because we were married did not mean we were not immune from the dangers of adultery. We witnessed firsthand how Satan wants nothing more than to break marriages and to destroy families, churches, and our gospel witness. In ministry, the stakes are higher, as an entire church can be ruined in one fatal adulterous blow. Throughout our marriage, we felt like we had a massive target on our backs. The spiritual warfare had never felt so intense before.

The process was painful, but we grew so much. I was challenged to submit to Josh and trust his leadership in areas that were scary to me. The Lord wanted me to trust Josh with the big things, like our marriage and everyday things too. For example, cutting my hair short or using glasses instead of contacts. The hardest was the time I had a skin tag on my ear, and Josh wanted to remove it at home with his knife. He assured me that he had performed these surgeries on himself and horses before, and it would save us money. I chose to trust God and his surgical procedure skills even though he had no medical degree. Ultimately, Josh feared the Lord and searched His word for wisdom, yet he was also human, so he made some mistakes along the way. Thankfully the skin tag removal procedure went well. However, the ministry didn't always go smoothly. Looking back we both confessed how much more loving and gracious we should have been. We soon saw that ministry was messy because people are messy and sinful—every single one of us, including us in leadership.

November 1, 2014

Dear Lovey,

I'm so thankful that you are my wife! I love you so much more than the time when we first met! And I am excited about all God has in store for us. He has blessed us—with so many things: children, a house, good cars, and what more could we expect from a God who freely gives all things to his beloved! I am also thankful for the various trials that are happening at church because I know that God will use it to purify and grow us and perhaps the church as well. Stay vigilant, guard the home-front, and keep watch over your soul and our sons at home.

Love, Hubs

November 13, 2014

There are no words to describe how in awe I am at your perfect match for me. Your character shines as one that helps me move away from my sins. I look up to you as a man of faith that I aspire to be like. I Hope that as the years pass I will be more like Jesus and like you. Thank you for modeling Christ to me. Thank you also for your forgiveness. Please excuse my sloppy writing… I am trying to soothe Nathan. By the way, you make handsome babies! I pray our marriage will grow stronger and sanctified.

Love, Wifey xo

God used Josh in our church to teach on sanctification and the importance of leadership qualifications. He took holiness in our own life seriously and taught on its importance for our gospel witness. He prompted the pastoral staff to go through the book *Holiness* by JC Ryle with a heart to grow in holiness himself and encourage others to do the same. Josh's biggest passion was Christ and the Great Commission. He felt it was his duty to not only preach the gospel, but to live it out and also to make disciples of others. He took discipleship seriously.

Josh used the ministry model from our previous church and implemented it. It consisted of prayer, leadership meetings, fun games, a time of worship with the musical accompaniment of talented youth, strong exegetical preaching, small groups, and social time with snacks at the end while the students waited to be picked up. Our youth schedule was packed. It was all more than just a program; it was our passion. In some ways, it was our life. In addition to our regular youth night, Josh put on events at least once a month and camps twice a year that facilitated relationships. He tried to balance fun outings with service projects and outreach events both for the youth group and church-wide. We also drove the church van and picked up local youth in the area that didn't have a ride or believing parents. This brought a good mix of churched and unchurched youth to our church.

God gave us a wonderful group of middle and high school students, most of whom we watched grow over the years. God also gave this special group of students a wonderful youth pastor in Josh that genuinely loved them and cared for their soul. Some students we saw graduate high school. Within the group, we had large families with multiple students, which translated into multiple blessings and opportunities. We even had the opportunity to minister to some in foster care. Some of these students we only had for a short season, while others were actively involved in that church for years. Noah was especially glad to be a part of the youth ministry at the eager age of nine. One of our sweet high school girls, Katelynn was also Nathan's nanny during our time in Kingman, and like an auntie to him. This ministry was not just a program to us. The kids became like our own. We were family. In fact, after Josh went to heaven, one of the young men in our group, expressed his sorrow to me and said, "Josh was like a father to me."

In addition to the joy the youth were to us, we also had an excellent volunteer staff that made our ministry possible. Most of our leaders were strongly supportive parents. We had two moms that did not lead small group, but were an immense help with logistics such as snacks, transportation, events, and watching Nathan so I could lead small group with the girls. One of the dads on staff regularly helped with worship and taught when needed. We also had several volunteers. Josh had a couple young guys that he worked with. The worship leader partnered with Josh from time to time. Although Josh played guitar and could sing, he encouraged the youth to get involved by leading worship. One youth staff member that was dear to my heart was a lovely young lady who came on board to be trained by me. I learned and grew so much through teaching her. At the end of our ministry there, this beautiful woman got married and asked me to do the devotional for her bridal shower. It was such a privilege and joy to witness her marry a godly man who served at his local church youth group too.

There was another college-aged woman to whom Josh and I ministered. Not only did we get to see her wedding, but Josh also performed part of the ceremony. It was another one of our most precious moments in ministry. Her husband was also named Josh, and her mom said he reminded her so much of Josh. I treasured this as I saw Josh model what a godly man is to these young ladies who would later choose a man to wed.

My beloved genuinely loved others, had integrity and was a God-fearing man who impacted others by his example. He made time even for those who were not in his flock. Josh was never about numbers and being the "cool" youth group. He focused on spiritual growth rather than numeric growth. Although he did seek to bring more students to share Christ with them, he never compromised the gospel for crowds. He refused to water down the gospel. Ultimately, Josh trusted in God's sovereignty and the power of the gospel to save. He believed Romans 1:16, "For I am not ashamed of the gospel, for it is the power of God for salvation to everyone who believes, to the Jew first and also to the Greek." We had several students profess faith in Christ during Josh's ministry. However, it was hard to tell at that early point if it was genuine saving faith that is not uprooted but withstands the test of time. On the flip side, there were also those students that Josh never got to see just how much of an impact he had on them. One student in particular was not interested in Josh's preaching. He was the social stud and was challenging to work with at times because he distracted others. This young man came to Christ not long after Josh went to heaven and revealed how influential Josh had been to his faith.

Similarly, sometimes I felt that I wasn't making a significant impact as only a wife. My husband was the one who held the spotlight and rightly so. He was the one who worked hard preparing sermons. He poured all his energy on the church and his flock. My job was seemingly small in comparison. I mostly dealt with housework, chores, and cooking. However small it felt at the moment, I now realize it was so much more. It was my privilege to pray for Josh and his ministry faithfully. He would confide in me. Josh took me with him to counsel couples or young ladies in which he would otherwise not be able to minister as effectively. There were times of weakness when I felt more of a hindrance than a help. God used even those moments to teach us perseverance. When I was discouraged, he cheered me on and vice versa.

Josh was good about reminding us of our God-given roles. With God's help, he lived out his headship role as a husband and gave me the opportunity to submit. Josh was open and honest with me in everything. If I was in the wrong, he gently reproved me. He frequently encouraged me in my ministry at home first, and then with the girls in the youth group. Josh graciously reminded me how to live out my faith practically. When he was feeling spiritually low, I reminded him of some of those same truths too. We were a dynamic duo together. Josh was inspired to write a poem about our partnership in ministry one rainy afternoon and asked for my help with it. It was titled, "Dynamic Duo."

January 28, 2015

My dearest love bug,

Right now you are sleeping in our room with Nathan, and I have just finished writing a poem that you and I worked on together. It turned out good thanks to your helpful insight. I love you so much. You are growing in Christ a lot, even more than you realize. Sometimes in the moment, we can't see the forest through the trees, but I am very proud of you and how God is working in your life. You are my greatest joy in this world, and I count it as one of the greatest privileges that I have ever experienced to be your husband. And I am looking forward to all that God is going to do up at camp and at Shepherd's Conference.

Phileo, Eros Kai Agape,

Hubs

February 1, 2015

To my dearest handsome hubs,

It is amazing that we are now nearly married for two years! I'm very blessed to grow together with you. The LORD is so wise to bring us together to be sanctified and to serve one another. My love for you, I realize, comes from God. I can't really be good, or shall I say an excellent, wife without God's help through the Holy Spirit, and yours as you shepherd me and preach His Word. I'm so glad for your job and for how to seek to honor Christ through our marriage roles. Even though it's painful, it's the best thing God can do. Thank you for serving Him and our family.

Lots of love,

Erika

Dynamic Duo

Sons of thunder, together we are
A dynamic duo to be sure
Hand and hand we onward go
Compelled by the gospels allure

Our partnership is in Christ
And it's His name that we proclaim
Yoked together by His love
And committed to spreading His fame

Like Paul and Barnabus we travel abroad
Carrying with us the good news
To family, friends, and wayward souls
That they might join us in the pews

To our task we both set our sights
Holding hands as we push the plow
Paring together in spreading the seed
For we've got a whole world to sow

Copyright Josh "J.D." Seibert 2015

[Chapter 4]

Duties of a Pastor and His Family

One question we were often asked was, "So what does a youth pastor do all day?" Some people have the mistaken impression that clergy sit around and do nothing. It could not be further from the truth. Josh was on call around the clock. As a youth pastor, his primary roles were preparing sermons, activities, and camps for the youth. There were endless other duties. His many other tasks included organizing family events, preaching once a month, counseling, making hospital visits, officiating funerals, retirement home services, local good news club, administration, leading worship, Bible studies, marriage classes, discipleship, meeting with local pastors, and praying at city council meetings. Besides all this, our church was constructing a new building without debt which meant all hands on deck. Josh was often called to work on his days off in areas he didn't feel gifted, yet was needed since we were a small church without enough talented people or resources to pay a professional.

Josh's schedule became overwhelming for us at times. The ministry quickly took over our lives. At first, I was jealous of the time and attention others took from my husband. I had to learn to view Josh as a gift offering to the Lord in his pastoral service. He did not belong to me but to God. Moreover, my husband was on loan from the Lord for His purposes. It was my privilege to be his helper. It was my job to free him up to fulfill his call to the ministry. The best way for me to do that was to tend the home front. The children and I still needed him too. However, his office was like that of a school principal that ruled the home by keeping us in check.

We both knew that to remain qualified for ministry our home life had to be in order. Josh was a man of integrity and took the elder's qualifications seriously because they are in the Bible. For him, that meant making time for our family too. When he was tempted to neglect time at home, I reminded him that we missed him. As a new pastor's wife, I often struggled to help Josh find that balance. Often I found myself wanting Josh home more than was feasible. I had a genuine desire to have a strong, exemplary marriage. We had seen other pastors sacrifice their marriage and families for the ministry. There was a part of me that caved into fear. It was a terrifying thought to imagine our marriage ending up shattered like the ones we witnessed break from the spiritual, emotional turmoil of ministry.

October 16, 2015

Dearest friend,

It is such a joy to be your wife, friend, and the mother of your children. I realize it is so difficult to adopt Noah and to become a dad and a husband at the same time. Thank you for being so brave to do it. And for being a good provider, father, and husband. We must keep fighting the good fight. Don't ever give up babe! You are doing a great job as a youth pastor. You will do a wonderful job as a senior pastor one day. Yes, you will always make mistakes, but you get right back up and try again. Never give up babe!

Love,

Erika

November 6th, 2015

Dear Love,

Thank you for being my constant and faithful companion. I couldn't think of a finner more committed person to do life with. I know that things are hard now with all the different difficulties that we have, but we have the hope of our faithful redeemer—the Lord Jesus. He will guide us, keep us, and direct our hearts till we see him face to face. I am so proud of you for all the strides that you are making in your fight against sin. Keep it up and excel still more. Our new pup Trey really loves you and has chosen to sit next to you while you scrapbook. He is a Godsent dog for our family.

Love,

Hubs

Josh loved the boys and me so much. Regardless of how tired he was, he'd find a way to get some play time with Nathan or attend Noah's baseball games.

Josh taught me that it was a privilege to be able to combine family time with work time within the ministry. Some of his work time was also family time since our family could go along. I had to learn to look at it that way. We got to do many things together in ministry. We sang at a retirement home every month, counseled as a couple, and the youth ministry was always a family venture. He was the pastor of our youth group, I was his assistant, and the boys were his sidekicks. He led the guys' small group and the discipleship of the male leaders and students, and I drove the discipleship of women. Even so, I treasured those times when it was just our little family together—or even better just the two of us. Josh committed to having regular date nights. A night out alone gave us an opportunity to connect without the kids or the church watching our every move. Quality time without others hovering over us strengthened not only our marriage; it helped our ministry.

In Kingman, we spent nearly three of our four years of marriage together doing youth ministry. It was where Josh and I grew closer to the Lord and each other as we learned to die to ourselves and to serve others. It was such a joy to do ministry together. We learned how to partner well. Josh was especially encouraged by seeing young men and women grow in the Lord. He felt blessed to baptize several of them.

We also experienced turbulent times those three years. These were times when the social fabric was changing hues. The debate on same-sex marriage was roaring. Josh responded to the priest advocating gay marriage in the local newspaper. His response got published in the paper.

A Brief Response to Father Leonard Walkers Article

"Gay Marriage-Making it Personal."

It was with a heavy heart that I read Father Leonard Walker's article entitled "Gay Marriage- Making it personal" in the Wed May 6th, 2015 edition of the Standard. As I read his words about Gay Marriage, I could not help but see if they were compatible with Scripture. I read with eyes not to judge or condemn, but eyes of discernment. Is Gay Marriage the same as Biblical marriage? From what Scripture reveals to us, the answer is unequivocally no. Gay Marriage is something completely foreign and antithetical to the Bible's teaching regarding marriage. I believe that Father Walker has proven this in his article which I shall demonstrate with a few excerpts from his column.

Truth is foundational to our thinking. "What is truth," Pontius Pilate asked Jesus long ago. That question is still ringing in our ears until this very day. For the most part, society has answered the question of truth by stating that it is relative to each person. It is summed up in relativistic sayings like "Your truth is not necessarily true for me, but I'm sure that it is true for you." The popular conception of truth is that it depends on the point of view of the holder and not in some objective external standard such as the revelation of God in Scripture. It is this truth that Father Leonard affirms when he states, "Not the sin of pride, but the virtue of living in the light of one's truth at any cost." Father Leonard's truth is his own truth, not the truth of the Bible, but one of his own making. His article makes it very clear that it is his own version of the truth that he applies to the issue of Gay Marriage, not Scriptures. I point this out because it is upon this version of the truth that his whole understanding of Gay Marriage is founded. But what did Jesus say about the truth? In Jn. 17:17 Jesus said, "Sanctify them in the truth, your word is truth." Jesus' truth came not from society, science, the media, social engineers or the Supreme Court, but simply from the inspired Word of God. Biblical truth is according to what God has revealed it to be in His inspired word. The truth about creation, the nature of man and even the truth about marriage. It is Scripture that Jesus points out is truth. Lest we forget, there is plenty that the Word of God says regarding the issue of homosexuality and marriage, i.e. (Matt 19:4-6; 1 Cor 6:9; 1 Tim 1:10; Rom 1:18-32). By his own admission, Father Walker, walks not in the light of Biblical truth, but has redefined truth as "Living in light of one's truth." We should not be surprised that with this redefinition of truth also comes a redefinition of marriage so that all might welcome a "the broader acceptance of marriage."

New faiths need new beliefs and symbols that give a visual representation of those beliefs. With Father Walker's new version of the truth about marriage comes a new atonement, new heroes of the faith and a reinterpretation of the historical symbols of Christianity. Father Walker's new atonement or shedding of blood, is not the singular atoning work of Christ on the cross, but an atonement of the blood of homosexual martyrs whose blood has paved the way for a "Broader acceptance of marriage." The once celebrated blood of Christ has now been replaced by the blood of the martyrs of the new faith of homosexuality. Hailing this new atonement, Father Walker states, "My marriage is founded on the sacrifices and the blood not just of the last ten or twenty years, but on the length of history itself. My freedom to marry legally today has been forged in prisons, death camps, gay bashings, murders, and executions which sadly still exist today." Though certainly, these are all atrocious, dehumanizing and contemptuous acts against humanity, they are not the atonement of the Christian faith, but the atonement of the homosexual faith. Notice that remarkably missing from this article is the celebration of the atoning work of Christ, which Father Walker has replaced with the atoning work of past homosexuals. Central to this new faith is a new atonement.

The Christian faith has its heroes of the faith (Hebrews 11). Men and woman such as the Apostle Paul, Peter, Jude, Mary Magdalene, Priscilla and Aquila, Justine Martyr, Tertullian, and Athanasius etc. Men and women who gave their lives for the truth of what Scripture affirms, not what it condemns. Who are the heroes of the new faith of homosexuality? Father Walker lists a few stating, "The modern heroes from Oscar Wild to Harvey Milk, from Richard Baker and James McConnel in 1970 to the couples still fighting the battles in states yet to legalize marriage. The list is too long to mention." It is imperative to note that these new heroes of Father Walker's faith are not Martyrs of the Christian faith, but martyrs of the homosexual faith. Men who in Walker's words bore the "blood, sweat, tears, and sacrifices made by those who have made this day possible." A new faith needs new heroes of its faith and these are found not in the pages of Scripture, the annals of Church history or Foxes book of martyrs, but in the homosexual movements own recent history.

This new faith not only has a new atonement and new heroes, but it also has new interpretations of historic Christian symbols. No longer is the rainbow a symbol of God's promise never again to flood the earth with water, or the triangle a symbol of the Trinity, but in this new homosexual faith they receive a new interpretation, one consistent with the metanarrative of its faith. Father Walker explains, "My freedom to marry legally today has been forged in prisons, death camps, gay bashings, murders and executions which sadly exist today. It is the history of the pink triangle to the rainbow." Social revolutions need their symbols to communicate their messages to those whom they would woo. Often times they take well known and historical symbols and simply reinterpret them to communicate their new ideas. This is exactly what the new faith of homosexuality does, it borrows from well-known Christian symbols and reinterprets them with their new truth.

So there is a new atonement, new heroes and new interpretations of symbols, is this not a new faith entirely? Not according to Father Walker who describes it as, "Faith that comes from God." However, is this faith the faith that Jude described as "the faith which was once for all delivered to the saints?" Is this the faith that Paul exhorted

Timothy to hold onto? Is it the traditions of Christ and the Apostles? Or is it a new faith perpetuated by what Jude describes as "certain persons who have crept in unnoticed." I would propose that a new atonement, new heroes and new interpretations of Christian symbols all argue not for the historic faith of Christianity, but for a new faith foreign to Historic Christianity but familiar to our ever-changing culture.

A Concerned Citizen of the Kingdom,

Joshua Seibert

In addition to his engagement with the community on biblical matters, Josh's concern for guiding the congregation to rightly thinking about the issue from God's perspective inspired his writing. In his effort to show his youth flock the absurdity of going against God's design for marriage between a man and a woman, he wrote a story. He wrote a short story about its faulty logic entitled, "If the Shoe Doesn't Fit, Wear It Anyway."

If the Shoe Doesn't Fit, Wear It Anyway

Wayne's entrance into the trendy shoe store was announced by a door chime as he stumbled across its threshold. The shoe salesman warmly greeted him and asked if he could help him find a pair of new shoes. Wayne cordially agreed, following the shoe salesman down an aisle stacked from floor to ceiling with all types of shoes. As the two men meandered down an aisle, the salesman couldn't help noticing that Wayne was having trouble walking, he was limping.

"Are you walking ok sir? It seems like those shoes are giving you a bit of trouble. I can fix that right up with a comfortable pair of new loafers," the salesman remarked.

"Oh, that would be wonderful," Wayne exclaimed, "These shoes are getting a bit worn out."

"Well, I'm sure that we can fix that and get you back to walking in no time. Here, sit down and I'll measure your feet, sir." Wayne complied, and the salesman brought over the foot measuring device to size his feet.

Upon measuring him, the shoe salesman noticed something quite queer.

"Sir," he exclaimed, "I've discovered the source of your limp...you have two right shoes on," he said while watching Wayne take off his shoes.

"Oh yes, that's right," Wayne said with a casual annoyance.

"Well, sir," the salesman continued, "I'm no podiatrist, but I can say right off the bat that is the source of your problem. Your limping is a result of wearing two right shoes when you have a right and a left foot."

"Limping? I don't limp, I walk," Wayne confidently asserted.

"Well, call it what you like sir, but I'd walk with a limp too if I tried to walk wearing two right shoes," the salesman remarked.

"Listen you," Wayne replied, "I didn't come in here to be given a walking lesson or be judged for how I walk. I came to get some new shoes. Are you going to get me a pair or not," Wayne demanded.

"Yes sir, of course. I'll get you a pair right now," the salesman replied reaching for a size nine of new penny loafers. "These should do the trick, sir," he said, opening the box and slipping the right shoe comfortably onto Wayne's right foot.

"Ah yes," replied Wayne, "that is a great fit! These are most comfortable."

The salesman then attempted to shod Wayne's left foot with the left shoe. "Ouch, what are you doing," Wayne cried, retracting his foot back as if he'd been electrocuted.

"I'm just putting the left shoe on sir," the salesman replied.

"I don't want a left shoe for my left foot! I want a right shoe for my left foot," Wayne protested.

"But sir, be reasonable," the salesman insisted.

"This isn't right. You can't stick a right shoe on a left foot. This sort of thing just isn't done. It goes against your foot's physiology and the very laws of nature themselves! Since the beginning of time, there has always been right and a left, up and a down, male and female, night and day. It is how the Creator has ordered the world. If you insist on going against the way that you were created.... well...You'll be imbalanced and...and...off. It's simply... unnatural."

"Quit philosophizing with me! If I wanted a sermon, I would have gone to church. Get me another pair," Wayne demanded.

Sensing the salesman's hesitancy, Wayne took the initiative by jumping up, seizing another pair of size nine loafers, and taking out the right shoe and then proceeding to jam it on his left foot. The salesman watched horrified as Wayne struggled to get the right shoe onto his left foot.

With a grimace and a grunt, the right shoe then slipped onto Wayne's disfigured left foot.

Amidst the struggle, the salesman inquired, "How did your foot get so disfigured?"

"Who are you, Colombo? What's with all the personal questions?" Wayne snapped.

"Well, I just noticed that your foot looks a little disfigured and I was wondering how long you've been like this," said the concerned salesman?

"How long I've been like what for?"

"Well, you know…insisting upon wearing two right shoes," the salesman replied.

Annoyed at having to explain himself to a shoe salesman, Wayne reached way back into his childhood years. "Well, you know when you are a child and you accidentally put the wrong shoes on the wrong feet?"

"Yes," said the salesman.

"Well, normally, when parents see this, they help the child realize their childish mistake."

"Go on…I'm listening," said the salesman.

"Well," Wayne continued, "Not my parents. When I was a young boy, I had lots of shoes, and one day I mismatched two pairs, putting on two right shoes. My parents, being the tolerant bunch that they were, didn't want to damage my budding self-esteem at such an early age, so they decided that the most loving thing to do was to not to say anything at all. After a few weeks of allowing me to do this, it just began to feel normal and my parents decided to accept me for who I was, a person with two right feet!"

"But you don't have two right feet" the salesman insisted, "You have a right and a left!"

"Don't judge by appearances," Wayne insisted, "I've come to accept me just the way that I am and all that I ask of the world is that it do the same!"

"But don't you realize that your insistence on wearing the wrong shoe is ruining your life? It is preventing you from walking how you were designed to walk. In fact, you are not even walking, you are limping through life. Walking with two right shoes is crippling you," replied the salesman.

"Well, that all depends on what your definition of walking is. I sir walk! Maybe not like everyone else, but it is walking none the less. Just because I don't adhere to your definition of walking doesn't mean that I don't walk. I would suggest that you expand your definition of walking to be inclusive of what I do," Wayne proudly replied.

The salesman, at this point had wearied of their conversation. "All right sir, if you say so…the customer is always right," the salesman reassured himself as he packed up the two left shoes in the box. "If those feel good to you sir, follow me, and I'll ring you up for both pairs of shoes."

"Both pairs of shoes!" Wayne gasped. "I don't want both pairs of shoes! I intend on buying one pair and one pair only. After all, what am I going to do with a pair of two left shoes?" Wayne protested.

"Well sir," the salesman responded, "What are we going to do with one pair of left shoes? You don't expect our store to take the loss, do you? Please be reasonable. You can't expect the shoe business to change the way that it operates just to accommodate your new way of walking. You will upset the whole order of the shoe business. People have a right and left foot, therefore we sell a right and a left shoe in a pair. This is the way that it has always been since man took his first steps in the Garden."

"Well, then I vote that we take the proper steps to change the created order! Where is the manager?" Wayne indignantly replied.

The manager, slurping a big gulp and watching the whole ordeal from the safe confines of a backroom on closed-circuit TV then came to the salesman's rescue. Addressing Wayne, he said, "Sir, you are more than welcomed to buy both pairs of shoes and do with them as you like in the privacy of your own home, but I cannot and will not sell you two right shoes. You either buy a right and a left, or two pairs of shoes. But I will not sell you two right shoes. Such a thing is just not done. If everyone started to do as you do, the world would end up as crippled and lame as you yourself are. I am truly sorry for your condition and what is happening to you. But sir, you cannot expect us to change the created order simply to accommodate your insistence on living outside of it.

"You will hear from my lawyer," Wayne replied, putting his old two right shoes back on and then stumbling out the door in a huff.

"Wow, my wife's always told me that when it came to dancing I had two left feet. But I've never heard of having two right feet," the manager remarked as he and the salesman watched their sale leave the building.

In the days that followed, the shoe store was slapped with a nasty lawsuit from Wayne's lawyer on the basis of discrimination. Weeks later, the two parties went to court where a judge ruled in Wayne's favor granting him a settlement of over 6 million dollars. Wayne became his own advocate, using his winnings to start a new lobbying group in Washington called "Same Rights for Same-Footed People" or SRFSFP for short. SRFSFP quickly became one of the most powerful special interest groups in the country. Its purpose was to reform the shoe business, expand the definition of walking in all creditable dictionaries and to advocate for same-footed awareness in the education system.

The shoe company didn't give up so easily, appealing the judge's decision, which then got held up in a string of applet courts for the next few years. These new trials received such publicity, that in the months that followed they triggered a national debate over whether or not the definition of walking should be redefined to include same-footed peoples. Wayne found himself an overnight celebrity and could be seen on all of the popular talk shows explaining and advocating for his lifestyle. He even got sponsored by Nike, who then pledged their support by issuing a new line of shoes called the "Waynester," sold strictly as pairs of left or right shoes. Jumping on the bandwagon, Hollywood celebrities began trying out the new trend and could be seen wearing only right or left shoes to show their support. The fashion world, never to be outdone, began to run their emaciated models up and down the catwalk with two same footed shoes. Slowly fashion began to overtake function, and the practice of wearing two of the same shoes became in vogue in both pop culture and the world at large.

In the years that follow, many shoe stores were forced to close their doors for refusing to accept the redefinition of walking and how they sold shoes. Some even experienced harsh persecution and social ostracization for clinging to the old order. Many simply went underground forging a black market for right and left shoes at swap meets and farmers markets. The culture besmirched these holdouts, labeling them, "dissentious," "out of step," "intolerant," "bigoted," "homopedia-phobic," "old fashioned," "backwards," and "haters." There was even a growing movement nationwide to enact legislation that would consider non-acceptance of the same footed lifestyle to be a hate crime, punishable by fine or imprisonment. Finally the revolution of what psychologist were now calling "Homopedia" or "same footedness" climaxed with the decision of the Supreme Court to hear the case. In a 5 to 4 decision, the court found that it was unconstitutional for shoe companies to sell pairs of shoes in only right and left and that to do so was an act of discrimination.

In the decades that followed, the culture stumbled along, hamstrung by their insistence on living outside of the created order. The cost of living in rebellion against their own physiology was incalculable, the loss immeasurable. By insisting upon living contrary to their biological makeup, mankind lost right and left, symmetry, balance, grace and poise. But most of all it lost a part of itself, what it meant to be human, to walk upright, erect and straight. With the world's institutionalization of same-footedness, mankind lost the simple ability to walk, handicapping many generations to come who would follow in their father's footsteps.

- Copyright Josh Seibert, June 26th, 2015

Strong ties got sewn at our church in Kingman. However, God made it clear to us that it was time to serve elsewhere summer of 2015. Josh was hoping to continue as a youth pastor in a church where he and the leadership would be more like-minded. God gave us the opportunity to candidate in Seattle for a youth ministry position. The senior pastor there was a God-fearing young single man. He encouraged Josh to pursue a senior pastorate role. At first, Josh was hesitant as he did not feel equipped for the responsibility of a church. However, this pastor reassured Josh that he didn't have to wait until he was glorified to pastor his own church. He then began thinking seriously about it. After much earnest prayer about the possibility of leading a church, he received the calling to pastor his own flock. He spoke of his desire to preach God's Word from the pulpit on a regular basis and feed Christ's sheep. Soon he started to search for senior pastor positions. Several churches called him back and there was one, in particular, that was on his heart in Southern Oregon. Josh's calling was also later confirmed by our loving church in Kingman where the pastor and the leadership ordained Josh.

During that last year that Josh continued to minister in Arizona, we saw how God transformed our hearts. Initially, we had been eager to go to a church with similar convictions—every week seemed so daunting. With each Sunday that approached we would nervously not know what to anticipate. At one point the pastor preached a series based on a book titled *Accidental Pharisees*. The premise of the book is about the danger of over-zealous Christianity that works itself out in legalistic ways. At first, Josh and I were taken back and felt personally attacked—especially since it was preached after Josh had addressed sin issues in the church leadership. After much prayer, Josh was able to step back and read the book with humility.

Josh did a great job of shepherding me through all the emotions

I had been battling against that had overcome me. It was hurtful to me personally that my husband was wrongly misunderstood. His zeal for holiness was a virtuous attribute. My husband was a man of integrity and his desire to call out continuous un-repented sin in the leadership was a result of his love for the church and commitment to God's Word. His heart was to honor the Lord, His Word and His people. However, my sweet husband taught me not to dismiss criticism, but to examine my heart for areas of growth. This was the way he personally approached the book and the pastor's preaching of it. He was such a godly example to me. By the end of the series, he said there was a good lesson we learned from the book. We learned that love, long-suffering, and humility are essential for the confrontation of sin. God taught my husband and me the importance of prayer and dependence on the Holy Spirit to sanctify our hearts and then those of others. It played out in our own marriage, and in our working with others in ministry.

Throughout that year Josh and I grew to greater love for our youth and the members of our church more than ever. It was a year of perseverance despite opposition. In the end, we felt we had tasted victory. The group had been well-established. Relationships with the students and our staff were flourishing. Josh had also learned to work well with others in church leadership despite differing views and convictions. He even worked with pastors from several other churches in town on joint ventures such a Thanksgiving service. Some challenges kept presenting themselves because of various opposing ministry goals and theological particularities. However, they were able to agree on the core gospel issues and proceed to the end that Christ's saving message of the cross be proclaimed.

The last day Josh served at College Park Baptist Church was the day he was also ordained as an official minister. It was such a joyful day for him, and it was also Nathan's second birthday. Although Nathan didn't get to celebrate his second birthday much that day, we later took him to Disneyland. We took a month off to spend time with family in Los Angeles before moving further away. On our drive up to Oregon, we stopped in Sacramento and visited the state capitol and several other museums, including the Train Museum. Nathan loved trains and was especially thrilled to see an entire children's section of Thomas the Train toys. It was one of our last family vacations.

April 12, 2016

Dearest Friend,

It's been a joy to grow old (a little) with you--both physically and spiritually. I'm so proud of you getting to be a more mature man. I also enjoy dreaming about the next journey or our life together. You will make a good shepherd and pastor. You have and are still learning so well how to be patient with people where they are at with the Lord. It has also been so refreshing to be able to laugh, cry, and confide in you through all we've been through. We are not fighting as much. The Lord has been so gracious to us both in growing us, and I trust he will continue to do so.

I love you most in all this world!

Erika, Xoxo

April 13, 2016

Hello, my Love,

Thank you for writing such a sweet note. This book is a wonderful chronicle of our love and feelings for each other and a testimony of God's faithfulness in our relationship. I thought it was cute to hear the story of how our little Nathan prompted you to write by bringing our pink book to you! I too am so looking forward to our next adventures together! Going to Merlin is going to be such a great opportunity for us, and I am so thankful for your continued support and encouragement. You are going to make a great senior pastor's wife. I love you so much!

Phileo, Eros, Agape,

Hubs

Hammer, Nails, and Wood

He was a carpenter by trade
Working hammer, nails and wood
Fashioning them together
As only a skilled craftsman could

Like a sculptor with his stone
Or a painter with his stroke
Christ fashioned earthly items
Chairs, a table or a yoke

But the mediums that He used
He'd continue to use still
And hammer, nails, and wood
Would be instruments that kill

From Carpenter to Savior
These crude mediums He'd not shirk
And with a hammer, nails, and wood
He'd accomplish His greatest work

Copyright Josh "J.D." Seibert 2016

[Chapter 5]

Preaching in Paradise Country

The quest to find the right church lasted an entire year. Josh meticulously approached searching for a new church. We traveled near and far—from short distances by car to visit churches in Arizona to getting on a plane and interviewing with churches in Washington, Nevada, and Oregon. The process of candidating was more complex than a simple work interview. For one church, we stayed with the pastor for an entire week. Josh was assigned to leading the youth group mid-week, preaching on Sunday morning, and being asked questions after church. In addition, they scheduled time to informally meet the leaders of the church. We were only given one free day for sightseeing and exploring the area. The interview process at that church was thorough which helped them wisely decide if we would be a good fit.

The lengthy process made it clear that this church would not be calling Josh to pastor the youth. Regardless, it was a great learning experience and we were grateful for our time with fellow brothers and sisters in Seattle. The pastor felt Josh was not called to teach youth, but adults. He encouraged him to seek out a senior pastor role. All the adults at the church in Seattle loved Josh, while the youth there didn't feel a connection with him. God used every shut door to better lead us to the one to which He would call us. Josh gave the suggestion to pastor his own church over to God in prayer.

Soon after, he felt the pull towards preaching and adult ministry. He started submitting resumes and the rest was history.

Early in 2016, Josh accepted the call to be the Senior Pastor at Merlin Community Baptist Church in a beautiful small town in southern Oregon. We had searched for a new ministry for nearly a year, though most of that time was in search of a youth pastor role. As soon as Josh sought a senior pastorate and saw Merlin Church, he kept this particular church fondly in prayer. Merlin Church had been searching for a pastor for about a year too after having their pastor of thirty years retire.

God made it clear for them that Josh was their next guy; even though they were searching for a long-term pastor and had no idea that God would call their pastor home in less than a year. God also made it clear to Josh that this church was the one. Merlin had been Josh's first choice based on location and church size. Once we met the warm and friendly congregation and saw their hunger for God's Word, Josh was sure it was where he'd want to spend the rest of his ministry life. Likewise, the elders and the congregation all agreed with a unanimous vote to call Josh as their new Senior Pastor.

Merlin Church was a perfect match for Josh. Oregon is an outdoorsman's Promised Land. It was like a preview of heaven for him. Ever since Josh was young, he loved to fish. He had always wanted to learn to fly fish. Whenever he had asked older men to teach him they simply said it was too difficult and refused to teach him. God fulfilled one of Josh's dreams by bringing our family to fisherman's paradise and having him learn to fly fish. The associate pastor, Mike Friend, had been a fly fisherman and was graciously willing to teach him. Josh quickly caught on to the art of fly-fishing since he had acquired the arm movement skill from roping as a cowboy. He soon took on the hobby of fly-fishing. It was his most effective stress reliever while serving as a senior pastor—his spoonful of sugar. Josh unwound from a busy day of work at our ponds on the ranch.

The Lord gifted us with Josh's dream rural home in a picturesque tucked away place called "Paradise Ranch." Our home was a cozy three-bedroom house with an office that functioned as our homeschool room. While it was no mansion, it was large enough to entertain the church. That is one thing we both had prayed for as we searched for a home. Josh knew he wanted to share our life with our new church family. This was just a way he sought to demonstrate that. He did not merely invite the church into our home but into our lives as well. Josh actually had the entire church over once for a Christmas open house. He felt the home was one of the most intimate places and that the congregation should be well acquainted with the pastor's home.

It was the first home we had with an official guest bedroom, which we enjoyed using to host visiting family and friends, especially since we were seven hundred miles away. We invited visitors from Los Angeles and even some from Germany. The best feature was that we lived on a 300 acre abandoned golf club development with four ponds on the premises. We could literally get lost exploring our own backyard. I had to use a whistle when I needed to call Noah for him to hear me. We enjoyed going on bike rides and hikes. As a family we took regular walks in our backyard.

Josh frequently fished. He took Noah with him, and they both enjoyed their time together outdoors. Daddy taught him how to put bait on the pole and gave him some pointers on catching fish. Nathan had a small fishing pole but was too young to go out with them. There were a few times he went and pretended to catch fish as he drew seaweed with his brother's small pole. Josh quickly made several fishing buddies that would take him out on their boat. They would go to the nearby lakes to fish, and Noah would tag along too.

Our new life in Oregon took off and we jumped right into ministry before Josh's official first day on the job. The church was excited and supportive in every way. They helped us unload boxes and gave us an early warm welcome. The beautiful home we rented on an abandoned golf course was a providence that God opened up for us earlier than anticipated. We had seen the beautiful landscape five months prior to actually moving. When we came to candidate and meet the elders, one of them showed it to us as a possibility. With few rentals in the area and growing high demand, there weren't many choices. As soon as we were told the church had voted to call Josh to be their next pastor, we tried to jump on the opportunity for the house. At first we were told it had just been leased and would become effective the beginning of April. The next day we got a call saying the person who came in to fill out a rental application did not show up or respond. We secured the property by renting the home a couple months in advance. Josh was supposed to start at Merlin in late July. We moved in June and figured we would just use the time to settle in and get to know our new church family. With Josh helping me to unpack and mount all our picture frames on our walls, we soon felt right at home.

Josh was eager to get to know everyone and dive into their lives. We had the chance to attend an outreach event before Josh's first official day on the job. It was an old car show where the church provided a free hotdog lunch, gave raffle prizes, shared a gospel presentation and invited the community to regular Sunday services. Josh was thankful for the church's shared heart for evangelism and reaching out to the community.

The town of Merlin is largely full of older retirees. Josh used the illustration of restoring an old car for his first sermon on the restoration work God does in the believer. It didn't take long for our family to warm up to the church congregation and vice versa.

They embraced us right away. Josh's love for his church was like his love for our children. He was instantly smitten. Josh's favorite term of endearment for the church flock soon became "beloved." His love was evident each time Josh preached. Almost every time he addressed the church he repeatedly affirmed his love with the word "beloved." And he truly meant it. Ministry was a labor of love for him.

It was a sobering responsibility, and one of the biggest blessings, for Josh to oversee and shepherd the church body. He took his role of pastor very seriously. Josh often prayed for the church with reliance on the Lord to help him lead His people. Sometimes, Josh went on prayer hikes and spent the entire morning praying for the church. Other times he prayed for members by name using the church directory. He also brought prayer sheets with specific requests home to lift up those needs. Josh prompted us to pray together as a couple for our marriage, the church, and our example to them.

June 27, 2016

My Dearest Love,

Thank you for your faithfulness to write in our book, it is a ministry of encouragement to me as well as a neat chronicling of our married life. I love you so very much and want to guard our marriage and the ministry that the Lord has given us. Please forgive me for not encouraging and cherishing you enough during the day. You are doing such a good job taking care of the home-front and mothering Noah and Nathan. I am also so proud of all that you did in our move to Merlin. It wasn't as stressful as it could have been due to your good planning and organizing. You also worked very hard in establishing our new home and finding new furniture on Craig's List for us, much like the Proverbs 31 woman, who is wise in what she buys for her household. I know that you miss our wonderful friendships and comforts of Kingman. Be assured that the God who was faithful to give them in Kingman will also provide them in Merlin. Please know that I am fully committed to loving you alone as my wife and friend and that I will take the proper steps necessary to honor both you and the Lord as your husband and the new pastor of Merlin Church. This is an exciting time of life for us and I would not think of anyone better that I'd like to spend it than with you my dearest love.

Phileo, Eros, Agape,

Hubs

Josh's biggest passion was preaching the Bible verse by verse from the pulpit. He also greatly enjoyed getting to spend personal time with individuals from our church and quickly integrated our family. Our sweet congregation embraced our children as their own right away. Our children and one other child were the only ones attending on a regular basis so they were spoiled by the many grandparents in our church that had relocated from their own grandchildren. In our spare time, we built on the relationships with our new church family. Among many things, Josh studied, wrote, taught, led meetings, counseled, networked with other local evangelical pastors, and still had time to train leaders of small groups and personal discipleship. For a short season, Josh was even able to study for sermons at home on Friday mornings. He watched the kids so that I could be a part of a ministry at the local pregnancy center. I joked that the kids gave him plenty of sermon illustrations while he studied. For example, when he was preaching from 1John on loving our brothers, the boys had been struggling with getting along.

From time to time Josh used personal examples during his sermons. However, Josh was careful not to put any of our family down with the illustrations he used. Shaming people was not something he purposed. Josh did not shy away from calling sin out, yet he refused to personally call people out in his sermons. He candidly dealt with general issues as they came up in the text. Josh favored expository preaching through books of the Bible. While at Merlin Church, he preached through First, Second and Third John. If an issue came up in the passage, Josh did not skip addressing it no matter how hard. He tried to bring uncomfortable topics to light in a way that shed hope to those struggling with sin.

Inevitably, the issue of church discipline came up, and the church did not know how to deal with it biblically. The issues that come up in Oregon reflected the culture in the area. The most notable was regarding marijuana use and the way it altered one man's ability to be self-controlled. A man in our church was smoking marijuana and causing harm. The sad thing was that he did not respond well to correction. His argument was based on a psychiatrist prescribing the drug. Josh had invested many hours with the gentleman and tried to lovingly reason with him using Scripture. It grew worse when he was unwilling to repent and defensively started calling all the church members to slander my husband.

There is nothing more heartbreaking than pouring sleepless hours, prayers, anxiety, and love into people and then having them turning around to bite the hand that fed them God's Word. Mind altering drugs only further complicate everything since they alter the perception of reality for that individual, and cause physical damage to oneself and others. After hitting a parked car and posing a physical threat to others, the man was asked not to return to the church premises unless he displayed some degree of repentance. God was gracious in that before Josh left this earth, peace was made and full restoration was given. The man kindly called him while he was hospitalized and asked for forgiveness, and was then welcomed back to the church.

Another issue that came up was over commercial surrogacy and IVF reproductive technology. It was a sticky one. Josh had never dealt with the issue before. Most of the church staff knew little about new reproductive technology other than the information that was given by the participants. Josh wrestled with it the more he read about in-vitro fertilization (IVF.) In most cases, an overabundance of human embryos are created, of which only few are intended to be brought to full gestation. An alarming number of embryos are thrown away or kept in limbo indefinitely or until they die out. According to the Medical Journal of Australia, "Of 1246 couples relinquishing frozen embryos, 1116 (89.5%) opted to discard rather than donate their embryos. Sixty-six per cent of donated embryos survived thawing. From donated-embryo transfer to 50 women in 92 cycles, a 17.4% pregnancy rate per transfer cycle was achieved, and 10 women delivered 11 healthy babies at term." On the surface the practice seems to promote life, but underneath the façade, it kills more life than it creates.

Josh spent much time listening to Dr. Al Mohler, president of the Sothern Baptist Theological Seminary, speak on the subject. In one article, Dr. Mohler says, "The excruciating pain of a married couple unable to achieve conception is understandable, but this does not mean that all technologies are therefore allowable or morally acceptable. Christian couples must not embrace the new reproductive technologies without clear biblical and theological reflection. At a bare minimum, Christian couples must commit to the implantation of all embryos, and the selective reduction of none. But this does not alter the fundamentally artificial character of the technology or the moral status of the embryos, and thus IVF presents grave moral issues to the Christian conscience. For these reasons, it cannot be encouraged" Al Mohler (Christian Morality and Test Tube Babies, Part Two. May 12, 2006).

Josh's heart was to expose the misleading campaign of the IVF industry and help the staff think through it biblically. Misunderstandings were used by Satan to further attempt to divide the church. At front and center was the inescapable reality that this particular surrogacy company, like the majority, made direct provisions for abortion. It was clear to my husband that this practice, as it was spelled out in their contract, was a violation of Scripture. Much time was spent on his knees, talking to other pastors, seeking counsel, searching for wisdom, researching the practice and the institution involved. Josh was convicted that the commercial surrogacy was not a practice that leadership should take part in while representing the church. In the end, the sweet couple involved was able to see the wrong aspects of the practice and their involvement in it. They courageously went before the entire congregation to read a letter asking for forgiveness for taking part in a commercial surrogacy. It was a hard yet beautiful thing to see God at work growing our leadership through this trial.

Both of these issues surfaced before our own personal trial with suffering commenced. It was good training ground for the biggest trial we would be called to endure. While it can be said that Josh's four years in ministry were the hardest, they were also the most joyous days of his life. Every now and then, I asked Josh if he wanted to take a break from ministry as I saw the physical and emotional toll it had on him and on our relationship at times. He resolutely refused. It was in the trenches of ministry that Josh and I learned the most valuable lessons in preparation for heaven. His eyes remained steadfastly set on seeking the impressable rewards from a life of sacrifice for the ministry.

Josh was committed to expository preaching, which was a new concept for the church. He lovingly and patiently cultivated a love for exposition in our new congregation. The people grew by leaps and bounds as the Word of God worked in their lives. Josh spent most of his time as a senior pastor preaching through the epistles of John. His heart was to remind us of the weighty and life changing message of the gospel. He spent about six months going through the first four chapters of Revelation. He also started a men's discipleship group with a few men from our church, including a Jewish man who gave his life to Christ as a result of their studies. The Jewish man attended church before with his wife, a strong born-again believer. However, he did not believe that Jesus was the Messiah. Josh studied the book of Matthew with the men and prayed for salvation. By God's grace, his Jewish friend understood the gospel and for the first time recognized Jesus as the Christ, and committed his life to Jesus Christ. It was Josh's upmost joy in this life to be pastor. He was blessed with the gift of shepherding his own church flock and leading several men to the Lord at Merlin.

Josh walked the church through his medical diagnosis and the topic of suffering. His last sermon series was on suffering and the sovereignty of God. He purposed to preach on suffering so that his own soul would be prepared to suffer to the glory of God and be an animated illustration to his flock. Josh taught on the origin of suffering and the purpose behind it. "...it is possible and actually God's desire, that we do more than merely survive or barely tolerate a season of testing or suffering. The Lord wants the experience, though perhaps difficult as we pass through it, to be a positive one in the end—one that strengthens and refines our faith." (MacArthur, 13). He sought to not only preach on suffering and God's sovereignty be to be a living example of how to suffer well.

The congregation was filled with mostly older saints. Some were in the midst of suffering through the pain of disease, on their last days themselves, or approaching that difficult season. Josh conducted several funerals while serving at Merlin Church and taught on the sanctity of life from the womb to the tomb, especially as it pertained to end of life issues. In God's providence, Josh was called to go down that same road and demonstrated by example how to live and die in a way that pointed people to Christ.

As a wife, it was my privilege to be Josh's helpmate in sickness and in health. I could either make his life bitter, or I could minister to him in his greatest need. By God's empowering, I chose to dedicate all my strength to help fortify him as much as it was in my power to do so. It was a struggle on most days. The Lord had to work in my own soul and teach me to grow in my attitude. My role as a pastor's wife was one of the most challenging I've ever been granted, and yet the most blessed. It was gut-wrenching to hear those we had poured much time and affection into slandering my husband with lies to try to discredit his ministry.

Having young children, my primary ministry was to my husband, my children and our home. This was all Josh expected of me. He also encouraged me to show hospitality. We often opened our home to others. When I desired to be involved with other women, he gave me the chance to be involved in the women's ministry and do a book study with some of the other female leaders. Josh was supportive of me using my spiritual gifts, but most importantly to cherish my personal relationship with Christ. Sometimes the best I could offer were my prayers, cheers, and encouragement.

Our church family displayed love and appreciation for the ministry God accomplished through Josh in a thousand different ways. The fruit that came from the short ministry we had together made it worthwhile. If I had the chance to marry Josh again, I would gladly do so. The Lord taught me immensely through our relationship and his example. We were best friends and could talk about anything, including ministry.

Josh gave all of himself in love, not only to me, but also to the Lord. Our marriage was the hardest yet the best experience of our lives. Although it wasn't perfect, we enjoyed the most intimate relationship both of us had ever known. Our love grew to a place of sweet harmony together. We learned to prefer one another, to be quick to seek and grant forgiveness, and diligently work on the areas where we fell short. This was our last writing exchange in our marriage diary, written before his diagnosis.

September 8, 2016

Dearest Friend,

I just finished reading the journals we wrote during our first honeymoon. It was so lovely to remember the joyous time we shared as we embarked on this journey of marriage together. It also brought tears to my eyes as I saw how awful I've taken our marriage and friendship for granted. Please forgive me for not loving and respecting you as I should. I wish I could be the fun, light-hearted, and attractive woman I once was. I work on it, but I fall so short. At least, I can be the prayerful, encouraging, and humble, woman who fears the Lord that God calls me to be. And I seek and beg Him for the grace to be that. You have done so much for me and have lain down your life in many ways for me and continue to do so.

You provide all our family needs. You always look for our good and protection. I'm proud of you as a husband, father, and pastor. Please forgive me for not viewing things rightly sometimes and allowing fear and emotions to pollute my mind and take their toll on our home. May the Lord nurture, protect, bless, and keep our marriage, home and children.

In Christ's Abounding Love,

Yours truly,

Mrs. Josh Seibert   xoxoxoxo

September 11, 2016

My Dearest Love Erika,

Thanks for being so faithful to write in our marriage journal and keep affirming your love for me and your Savior. I am so encouraged by all the spiritual progress that you are making and how you are growing and maturing in your faith. You are so courageous to start this new study at the pregnancy center, and I just know that God is going to use the study powerfully in your life to encourage and affirm you as His beloved daughter. I am so enjoying our new home up here in Oregon with you and our family. Thank you for being understanding and letting Noah and I fish so much. It really is very therapeutic for both of us and gives us some good bonding time. I miss our date nights, so we will have to take the church folk up on their offers to baby sit so that we can get some much needed date time. Please forgive me for not appreciating you enough and encouraging you and our family. I am trying to be more of an encouragement to you and am praying to do so.

Love Always,

Hubs

Josh humbly wanted to serve in Merlin for the rest of his life, which he did. He just didn't realize how short that would be. Josh's doctor had run a random set of blood tests to check on his historically low thyroid. The results showed low blood counts in addition to his expected low thyroid levels. The doctor suggested Josh see a blood specialist regarding his low counts. However, the doctor didn't think it was a big concern. He merely told us Josh would likely take medication for the rest of his life to remedy the problem. We didn't have medical insurance at the time, so we decided to wait till we got settled in Oregon to see the blood specialist. Perhaps we should have gone to see a specialist sooner. Maybe. Either way the result would have been the same.

God tells us in Job 14:5 that we cannot pass the boundary of how much time we borrow upon the earth, and in Luke 12:24 that we can't add a single hour to our life by worrying about it. God had us where He wanted us for a season. Josh's disease had progressed beyond the average life expectancy of it. The brevity of his time on this earth, as a husband and father, as a son outlived by his parents, as senior pastor in Merlin, was all for reasons only known to Him. We trust the turn of events that followed as having been lovingly ordained for the good of God's people.

Christ's Bride the Church

I see the church clothed
In her snow white gown
With every angle hushed
They dare not make a sound

She stands poised
Pure and complete
Ready to cast her crowns
At her husband's feet

Every tribe, tongue and nation
From the dawn of creation
Waits with anticipation
For the church's consummation

Christ purchased His bride
By laying down His life
He came to the world
To take Him a wife

So let us partake

In the marriage feast of the lamb

For your husband to be

Is the great I Am

© Josh Seibert

Chapter 6

From the Pulpit Stand to the Hospital Bed

J osh made inroads into people's lives quickly. He soon gained traction with church members and member of the community, and Josh wanted to keep the momentum going. He joyfully juggled the challenges of ministry and family. He naturally became physically exhausted. His previous doctor had recommended he see a hematologist to help him with the fatigue, which we attributed to his low thyroid levels and a stressful job. We didn't schedule an appointment until three months after Josh had started his new position as Senior Pastor, once we were settled in Oregon. A bone marrow aspiration indicated some alarming results.

The sterile clinic still vividly comes back to mind. I can clearly remember the look on the young woman's face when Josh and I walked in. He had already seen her and given me a report with names of possible diagnosis. I had spent quite some time trying to understand and research everything I could on the possible diseases, prognoses, and treatments. She was a young beautiful blonde woman who spoke with a Russian accent. The doctor kept saying she didn't exactly know what the diagnosis was but that it was very peculiar. She told us results indicated the possibility of either Aplastic Anemia or Myelodysplastic Syndromes (MDS) with the latter being the worst of the possible diseases. She explained why upon further testing, they thought it was most likely MDS. However, she told us they could not pinpoint it because of unnatural characteristics of his biology. She offered to run more testing but could not guarantee any further answers. We had already received a bill of over ten thousand dollars in tests, so we politely declined. We left frustrated. How could someone with the title "specialist" have so few answers? She referred us to the Oregon Health and Science University four hours north of us for further testing. Some of our family wondered if medical students could offer any more answers. I earnestly prayed they would have answers and way to treat whatever he had.

Shortly after the referral, Josh received a call from the university saying they wanted to see him right away. He was scared because of the concern in their voice. They were very sympathetic and offered to admit him into the hospital the next day, so they could expedite his testing. At first, he wanted to drop everything and rush over to be admitted. After thinking it through, he decided to wait. Finances and hospital coverage was a big question mark. Josh already had a busy work week ahead and pending responsibilities. He called his friend who worked at a hospital doing billing. Then, called our friend who practices medicine. After counsel from friends and prayer, he decided to apply for financial aid first and wait to go in as an outpatient.

The next hurdle we had to overcome was learning our insurance, which was a Christian co-op, would not cover anything because it was a pre-existing condition. The news seemed to be going from bad to worse just when we thought it couldn't possibly get any worse. It was at this time we drew upon the promises of God's goodness (Romans 8:28). We prayed, along with hundreds of others. I started an online fundraiser to help raise financial support to cover our medical bills. The Lord faithfully provided the funds to pay thousands of dollars in bills that had already accumulated. Furthermore, we were able to get a scholarship from the hospital for all needed procedures except a million-dollar bone marrow transplant. We praised God and got Josh an appointment as soon as possible. Since the scholarship didn't cover a potential bone marrow transplant the next step was to attempt to apply for medical insurance too. Providentially, we were able to apply for insurance the following month since, in God's providence, it was open enrollment for coverage for the upcoming new year.

There was some waiting time in between since it was mid-November, for which Josh was thankful. He was not immediately ready to move forward with such a risky procedure or the reality that death could be imminent. While we waited for confirmation of a diagnosis, we hoped it was all a mistake. Both of us needed time to process what was surprisingly happening before our eyes. Below is my last journal entry in our marriage journal. It was written to my beloved shortly after we both got the news that Josh's disease could be fatal. Josh did not reply or write in our love journal after this. He began to grow distant, yet not in an unkind way. Josh may have been grieving or trying to protect me from a more severe impact if death hit. He must have wondered how devastating it would be for me to lose him. At this point, we didn't know the cause of his MDS or how bad it was. The one thing we knew about MDS was that in severe cases a patient could die within five months. Josh asked me with a straight face one night, "Erika, what would you do without me?"

November 11, 2016

Dearest Love in all this earth,

It breaks my heart to think of losing you. I love you so much more than I can tell you. You are my kinsman redeemer. I see you are a godly example to me of what it means to be selfless, wise and mature in the Lord. I can't tell you how happy I was that you not only took notice of me as a single mom but would not give up in pursuing me and did not hold any bitterness toward me. Also, still today you do not hold bitterness toward me for too long. Once you forgive me, you honestly see me as the same as before I sinned against you. I wish I were better sanctified in my meekness, submission, and kind responses. I know that I can do all things through Christ who strengthens me. You can live the last however many years God gives us, in sweetness, joy, and fun with the boys. Noah now is as much your son as he is mine. He got despondent when you told him you might die. You can live another 20 years; I really hope so. We don't know why this is all happening, but we know God is allowing it. I pray God gives you the grace to endure this trial, the wisdom to make the right health/medical decisions, and the kindness to make the most of things. I trust you will, and I am so proud of all you have done in the past four years.

Love, Erika

Three days after his 37th birthday on November 29, 2016 Josh was diagnosed with a severe case of his Myelodysplastic Syndromes (MDS) and generously given—at most—up to a year to live if left untreated. The only possible cure for his MDS was to undergo a risky bone marrow transplant, which could buy him a decade or two more of life. They told us the success rate for the procedure was at 40-60 percent and likely on the higher side since he was young.

Josh had a pastor's heart and kept others in his prayers, even amidst his pain. He was an exemplary example to his family and the church of entrusting himself to God even in his suffering. In his last days, he was sure he needed to be near his beloved church. Although doctors had suggested we move back home and be treated at UCLA to be close to family for support, he knew he needed to stay in Oregon to serve his ministry until whenever God called him home. He once said, "I will die in the pulpit." Josh wanted to be there to support the church, and in the end, the church supported our family more.

On New Year's Eve, we got a call that confirmed that his MDS had been a result of a rare genetic disease called Fanconi Anemia (FA), which is incurable and makes patients much more susceptible to cancers and unable to handle chemotherapy. We had taken a family road trip to be with family in Los Angeles. On New Year's Eve, we were at his parents' house, and his extended family gathered together. Josh shared his FA diagnosis with everyone there. Then he shared how God had given him peace from his faith in Christ. He knew he would likely die, and heaven would be his destination. When we said goodbye on that trip, Josh and his family wept as if it were a final goodbye, and for his niece and nephew, it was. It broke my heart. I was still in denial and wanted everyone to stop crying and see that there was hope for Josh to live many more years ahead.

Before returning to Oregon, we enjoyed our last family vacation together. We visited Battleship Iowa. That day, I remember Josh was having trouble walking through the narrow stairs of the ship. At one point he had to stop from feeling dizzy. His health was already starting to take a turn for the worst.

We were nearly 700 miles away from family back home and had to relocate another four hours north from our church family for the transplant. I decided to create a blog to chronicle our incredible journey (www.ThisThornyRose.com). This is the first blog entry. More followed and recounted our journey through the thorns that God used to bring about a beautiful rose for His glory.

January 20, 2017

Our journey as a family through this difficult trial has merely begun... We have come to terms with the reality of what's going on. At first, we had hoped Josh's diagnosis was just a mistake. Then, every time we got news from a doctor, it seemed to get worse and to confirm the gravity of his disease. The first few days we just sobbed together. Then we told our closest friends and loved ones, and they cried with us.

Later, we broke the news to many more—our church, extended family, and our friends via social media. As more people found out, we sensed people were praying for us. We were encouraged by others and received supernatural peace despite the seeming hopelessness circumstance. Josh has a wonderful sense of humor that can lighten any gloom. He even jokes and sings hymns about his death. At that point, I tell him to stop!

As suggested by a friend, I created a fundraising site. I shared it on Facebook to see how others would respond. To our astonishment, within days thousands of dollars were donated and medical bills paid in full. This was so encouraging! It helped lift the financial burden off of Josh's shoulders. The day of our first appointment with the transplant team, we met a sweet local Christian lady who offered to help. As we begin planning for the unknown future, we believe that God will continue to provide for all our needs including things out of our control like a 'perfect match' donor. I have spent nearly every waking hour and sleepless night researching Josh's disease and possible treatments. Now, more than ever though we will need to cling to Jesus and trust him with every detail. We will need to stay close to Him with every step we take ahead.

The blog was an excellent channel God used to journal the road of suffering we traveled. Through it, we played back the scenes when we felt like we were falling from the edge of a cliff with only a thin thread holding us and see the ways God upheld our faith. It was a time of intense fear. God supplied the needed faith to carry on each day. From the beginning, time after time, God proved faithful to provide what we needed in the nick of time. God displayed His hand throughout the stormy voyage and gave us a gentle calm in the middle of the chaos.

We each tried to cope in our own ways. Noah doubted Daddy would make it. Nathan was emotional. I had to be strong with high hopes, while not completely naïve. In the back of my mind, I told myself of the reality that death could be waiting around the corner. At the same time, my aching heart wanted to deny the gravity of the situation and hold on to hope that Josh would pull through. The fact that he might not make it caused us to cherish each moment like never before.

February 10, 2017

Yesterday was a busy day. We drove from Grants Pass four hours north to OHSU in Portland and back for what was supposed to be only a two-hour bone marrow transplant class that had morphed into a full day with back to back appointments. We got more familiar with the campus as we had different places to go for almost every appointment. However, we experienced much grace and blessings out of it.

The first blessing was Josh getting to pray for a 29-year-old man in our transplant class with three kids (including a 9month baby!) They will likely be in the hospital together for the transplant. Secondly, we got a lunch break where Josh and I got to go on a 'date' to a local cafe close to where we will be staying in Portland. Thirdly, we got to pray for a Christian couple expecting their second daughter. Their names are Eli and Shannon. They were waiting to find out what was wrong with their baby as they had found fluid in her head and problems with her heart.

Please pray for them. We were heartbroken to see all the sick and suffering children in the children's hospital side. We are thankful not to be in that position of seeing our children sick like that. Fourthly, even though the 'breathing' team requested to have Josh get a transfusion due to meager hemoglobin count (which affects your oxygen), he didn't end up getting one. We are praying he won't need one, and that he be as healthy possibly before transplant. Lastly, we got to do all this without having to bring the kids. We have a supportive church family help care for them for the day. There were countless other little ways the Lord showed us kindness throughout the day.

Now, we continue to plan for transplant. We drive back to OHSU every week until they finally admit him. Josh has two full days back-to-back of more pre-transplant routine appointments next week. We are going to need to spend a night or two in Portland. Our anniversary is next week too. We are hoping to go out for dinner to celebrate the sweet times we've had in marriage, and the amazing work of sanctification God has done in only four years. We just got a call from a social worker who found out we needed to spend two days up in Portland. She 'happen' to offer us an available room for two nights during our anniversary at a nice hotel for free! That floor in the hotel is usually only for patients' families who have kids in the hospital, which surprised me. God continues to show us his loving provision every day.

As transplant nears, it's been tempting to become anxious and fearful. Please continue to pray for us to have peace and rest in God's care and lovingly wise hand over every aspect of our lives.

Josh's health was already plunging. A few weeks before his transplant, he needed a blood transfusion to keep him going. I remember finding ourselves in the hospital chairs astounded that he was in need of someone else's blood to sustain him. We were worried and asked our medical team if it would affect his transplant to which they assured us just one blood transfusion would not hinder his transplant. They insisted, saying it would make a positive difference in keeping his blood count where it needs to be in preparation. The evening after his first blood transfusion, he wanted to enjoy his favorite pastime—going thrift store shopping. We ended up at the largest Goodwill outlet stores we've ever set foot. I could not get him to stop shopping. He had so much energy! Part of me just wanted to sit him down. I grew concerned that if he used too much exertion, his battery would run out and he would need more blood. That night he was like the energizer bunny.

February 17, 2017

Our latest visit to Oregon Health and Science University (OHSU) was more delightful. We had more time to relax and not feel as pressured to go-go-go. God is so kind and gracious. We only spent half the day at OHSU on Thursday which was very refreshing. Josh had wanted to get together with one of his friends, and we got to spend some time together by visiting his workplace and eating a late lunch there together.

Later that evening we also got to celebrate our anniversary by having a romantic dinner at a restaurant on the 30th floor overlooking Portland. It was beautiful! The only downer to our lovely evening was accidentally getting stuck in an underground employee parking garage. I almost had a panic attack. Instead, I prayed, got out of the car, and took a deep breath of fresh air. We need prayers that I'd be tough. Josh said God might be trying to help me toughen up. I'll probably laugh about this incident later. However, for now, it was a good learning experience of being in a stressful situation and the importance of praying and staying calm. Praise God for the Holy Spirit who gives us peace and helps! We eventually did manage to 'escape' after what seemed like an eternity but was only about 5-10 minutes. An employee came in to park his car and got us out. There will surely be many highly stressful times during Josh's treatment, so it was kind of like a little drill.

When we got back, we were able to relax in the hot tub at our hotel. It was so amazing because we ended up getting to know the only two other families that came into the pool/ spa area while we were there. They were both families that love the Lord! What are the odds, in Portland, for three Christian couples meeting at a spa at the same time? It was a divine appointment. We had an instant connection. We got to pray with both of the families and were encouraged by one another. They are both going through medical issues at OHSU. One of the husbands there was also a pastor, and Josh enjoyed a long conversation with him.

Friday, we spent most of all day at the hospital. We rode the sky tram at OHSU in between appointments, just for fun. Also, we took a long enough break to run a quick errand and have a lunch date. We found a cute local diner, walked around with no rain, and even got some sunshine. Then, we still managed to sneak into a sweet French pastry shop where we enjoyed gluten-free desserts.

Along with routine labs and check-ups, Josh saw a physical therapist and his transplant doctor. It was a good visit with his doctor, but she informed us that Josh's blood counts were down dramatically and would need a blood transfusion. She reassured us that it would not negatively impact the transplant since he doesn't have transfusions frequently. It was his first time having a blood transfusion so it was scary, but the doctor assured us Josh would feel much better and energized afterward– and he did!

God showed us His kindness in leading us to the university where the Fanconi Anemia (FA) Fund started, one of the best places in the country for its diagnosis, OHSU. At that time, the average life span for someone with FA was only 33 years old. Josh died at age 37. I was thankful to God for the four extra years He gave Josh. Those are the four years I had with him. God didn't have to give me any time with Josh, but he did. I praise God for that time and would not trade it for anything. Those four years taught me a great deal about depending on the Lord. In addition to Josh's diagnosis, my dad had just been diagnosed with prostate cancer. It seemed like our world was falling apart before our eyes. Thankfully we ended up finding out my dad's cancer was only at stage one. Still, it was a season of intense testing and having to lean on the Lord's grace and provision fully.

The Lord provided for our Josh's treatment in many tangible ways. He used His people to help. Merlin Church stood with us all the way—holding Josh's position and granting him a paid medical leave. We needed to be in the heart of Portland. OHSU required that we live within twenty miles of the hospital to accept him for a transplant. It was a challenge to find inexpensive housing in the city, on top of keeping up with our rent in Merlin. We reached out to like-minded churches in the Portland area asking for help. A sweet Christian lady who lived in a cute antique home saw our need. That night she dreamed of a boy crying for help and called us the next day. She was close to the hospital and offered her home to share with us. However, she had a three-story house with too many steps for Josh to climb post-transplant and no yard for the kids to play.

We trusted God would work out the kinks and even moved a couple of items into their home a few weeks before our scheduled move. The week before Josh's transplant, we got two calls. One was from the dear lady offering to share her home with us. Her daughters had friends from out of the country visit the week Josh went in for the transplant, and we needed to find another place for that brief time lapse. The other call was from Clackamas Bible Church with an opportunity to affordably rent a spacious three bedroom missionary house with a small yard on campus. Josh wanted our family to be surrounded by the church for their moral and spiritual support, and this is precisely what the Lord provided. The cost was minimal and we were reimbursed later.

Besides the provision for temporary housing, God also gave us the perfect caregiver for our children. A mature young lady named Katelynn from our youth group in Arizona offered to live with us to be a nanny for the boys and provide the needed love, care, and stability for them. The boys already knew her well. Little Nathan absolutely loved her from the weekly times she would play with him during youth group nights. Instead of having to recruit random people from the church to trade shifts to watch the kids, they were blessed to have the same person look after them consistently. She was instrumental in freeing me up to be by Josh's side to encourage and advocate for him at the hospital.

Things were lining up well in preparation for the transplant. We weren't sure what to expect as far as donor matches. The doctors said it could either be extremely difficult to find a close match or Josh could have many to choose from—it just depended on his genetic make-up and potential matches from the national bone marrow registry with "Be the Match." This wonderful organization also awarded us a scholarship for some of the transplant costs, which was so helpful.

On top of having our own home and caregiver, we heard news of a perfect-match bone marrow donor. First, we received the great news that Josh had 15,000 potential matches in the database. His medical team spent some time evaluating them for the best possible one. They pinpointed the donor they wanted and contacted him to see if he'd be willing. We anxiously waited to hear his response.

February 22, 2017

Our family has been very busy trying to prepare for Josh's upcoming transplant. God has been preparing our hearts and the children's. We praise and thank him for the blessings we see along this bumpy journey.

We had the opportunity to host a team from Germany that was on tour in the western part of states helping Fanconi Anemia (FA) patients screen for mouth cancers, as FA patients are more susceptible to throat and mouth cancers. They joined us for dinner and stayed the night at our home. We had the chance to ask them lots of questions. Their story of how they ended up doing what they do was touching. Ralph, the leader, lost two young daughters to FA. We enjoyed getting to know them and learning the German way of life. Noah was surprised that they also use cell phones like us. Talking to them helped us get an idea of what we're fighting against and what to expect.

The team took a look at Josh's mouth and said he looks outstanding. Praise God! We hope it stays that way even after bone marrow transplant (BMT.) They also looked at his numbers for hemoglobin, blood cells and platelets; and they were concerned about how they are steadily decreasing. It's good that Josh will have a BMT soon. The concern is that his MDS may quickly turn into Acute Myeloid Leukemia (AML). AML is much more difficult to treat and is deadly. Prayers for Josh's disease not to progress are much appreciated.

We are waiting to hear back from OHSU on Josh's donor to confirm the date for his bone marrow transplant. Josh's doctor put in a request that asked his donor to give some of his actual bone marrow and not just stem cells. So we are praying that God would move his heart to say yes! We pray and wait.

God answered this prayer with a resounding yes. The donor was a 23-year-old sizeable young man who was not only willing to give his stem cells but his actual bone marrow. This was the next best thing to an actual sibling match. Josh just had one sister, and she was battling health issues at the time. It was a problematic medical process to navigate. Josh did much research and made the decision himself to have the transplant done after much prayer and consideration. We did everything humanly possible regarding lining up the best possible treatment that God provided for; it was now time to rest in God before heading off to fight for his life. The week before being admitted into the hospital, Josh's family surprised us with a visit.

When We Tally the Sum

When we tally the sum
In years to come
Amidst grey hair and wizened brow
One can't help but hope
That the grander scope
Will prove worthwhile somehow

In action and deed
In want and in need

[102]

Marriages' vows still preside
With ourselves the price
Of this sacrifice
As Christ was for His bride

And while time moves on
And our youth is gone
Our hope grows younger still
For a concluding story
And a future glory
That ends with the Father's will

And the lives we live
And the love we give
Are what becomes our legacy
For it's those that last
When the time has passed
And embraced eternity

Copyright J.D. Seibert 2008

[Chapter 7]

The Fight for Life

Josh fought for his life with all his strength and might. He loved our family and the church God gave him to shepherd. He did not want to leave us all behind. It would have been much easier for him to have opted out of any treatment and not go through with the bone marrow transplant. In fact, at first, that's what he initially wanted. Josh hated hospitals and would much rather have died while preaching in the pulpit or asleep at home. However, the more he prayed, studied Scripture, and talked to other pastors, he knew he could not go without a fight for life. The day my beloved got admitted into the hospital was surreal. We had been busy working hard to get him in as soon as possible. The cancer was aggressive. A failing bone marrow would leave his body depleted of blood and in constant need of transfusions. Soon, he would be unable to get any more needed blood from iron accumulation.

March 10, 2017

I think we are all in a bit of a shock right now. Josh was admitted into the hospital tonight. We knew it was inevitably coming, but now it is a reality. Upon departure from our little home away from home, Nathan cried when Josh said goodbye –he wanted to go with daddy. Watching him cry made my emotions want to explode. I had to hold it together. When I got back home, Katelynn, our live-in nanny assured me he stopped crying a couple of minutes after we left. She has such a heart for the boys and keeps them grounded. She is a rock to them while we are away. The hospital unit highly monitors for infectious control. Since I plan to visit daily, I have to wear a mask everywhere I go. It is a small sacrifice. Josh has to put on a mask, gown, and gloves to merely walk out of his room within the hospital halls. Please pray for him to adjust to his new 'foreign' environment. It is not pleasant, but Josh is making the best of it. Today, he smiled and said they got the best ice–he loves his ice and cranberry juice. He still has a sense of humor. Josh makes the staff laugh at his silly remarks and funny jokes. I'm sure he will end up with many new friends. He got to pray for the guy who delivered dinner to his room tonight. The primary goal today was to get him hydrated in preparation for tomorrow. Chemo treatment starts tomorrow morning. Please pray for Josh as he endures the 4-5 days of chemo ahead. The nursing staff assured Josh of being able to anticipate and relieve most of the awful symptoms associated with chemo and medications. Pray for Josh to remain steadfast and to be a light that would lead others to Christ.

The hospital was a constant reminder of Josh's serious condition as well as the effects of sin and living in a broken world. We met several patients that had little chance of making it out again. Unlike ever before, the brevity of life hit us. We had no idea if Josh would come back home to us. We were thankful to God for the hospital's caring team of professionals and appreciated like-minded conversations with some of the staff. God placed believers in our path that inspired us and vice-versa. One of them was the hospital chaplain. Josh found much encouragement from reaching out to others in the cancer ward. It helped when he could take the focus off his suffering and think about what others were going through—most of whom had no true and lasting hope.

March 13, 2017

The most heart-wrenching part of Josh's treatment has begun as we see some of the side effects of chemo kick in and Josh's numbers drop. It looks like it's going to be a scary set of ups and downs and a roller coaster of emotions. Josh completed his third out of five days of chemo today and has hardly gotten any sleep. He is starting to feel sorely exhausted. One of the side effects of hydration, which is essential for chemo, is the overflow of fluids swelling his body and even causing breathing problems. Some of that fluid went into his lungs last night. They addressed the issue and got him feeling better this morning.

"Thank you Lord for your quick answer to our prayer and using the doctors to help Josh! Please, Lord, enable Josh to get through this transplant and grace him with as little side effects and complications as necessary."

Despite all of these side effects and exhaustion, Josh is still relentlessly praying for others around him—making others smile with his sense of humor—so much so that that I worry he may wear himself out. He finds much joy in ministering to others at the hospital. Before being admitted he said it would be his goal to be like the hospital Chaplin. That is what Josh's mission has been. We prayed for a believing couple today who are also in treatment while doing laps together. We'd appreciate your prayers for God to give Josh strength to be able to reach out to others and stay active while still pacing himself.

The kids got to see Daddy on Sunday afternoon, and that was very special to all of us. We had to wear ridiculous looking masks to church that morning. That was a real challenge for the boys. I'm thankful to God that they are healthy during a season where it seems like everyone is passing around bugs and colds. The isolation part of all of this makes things complicated with a family and social children that yearn to make new friends.

The hardest thing for me as a wife is being unable to stay by husband's side twenty-four hours a day. I do get to visit him every day, and I'm thankful for that time. It makes Josh happy too. I'm grateful for Katelynn watching the boys while we visit. Josh has wisely wanted me home to give our children the mothering they need during this troublesome time. Even though I know this is the best thing for them, it still breaks my heart not be there for my hubs at every hour of the day. I long to be by his side if something goes wrong in the middle of the night. I can't imagine how terrible it feels to be in a hospital room for so long, trying to sleep through noisy machines and nurses checking on you periodically throughout the night. Prayers for Josh to be able to sleep better are also much appreciated. Lastly, please pray for me to keep myself from drowning in waves of uncertainty, fear, and sorrow that continuously threaten to overtake me.

Josh appreciated me being by his side at the hospital, but he selflessly wanted even more for me to be there for the boys. At first, he only allowed me at the hospital for a few hours per day. He carefully planned to increase my time away from the kids as they adjusted with their live-in nanny Katelynn. We all saw the benefit of stability for them in having me close, especially since they might lose their dad. At the same time, my beloved need me too. He had no one else there. His family was in Los Angeles 700 miles away. Our church family was in Southern Oregon 250 miles away. He was alone for hours at a time, confined to bare hospital walls, and bombarded with loud machines. I just wanted to snuggle by his side and stay with him throughout the night as we had done nearly every night since we got married. I felt torn. What if something happened to him while I was gone?

March 14, 2017

This morning when I tried to call Josh, he sounded drowsy, and all he said was that he couldn't talk because he didn't feel well and had to go. So I got on the phone with the nurse and asked her for an update. She said Josh had a rough night, had to be put on oxygen, and had a fever they were trying to reduce. She said he was ok now. Frightened by the thought of my husband on oxygen, I asked her if his symptoms were typical side effects of the chemo. To my relief, she said yes. Noah was concerned about daddy, so we prayed for him. Nathan wanted to set the table for daddy when we ate. I kept telling him daddy would not be joining with us today. Not taking no for an answer, Nathan said it would be for when daddy came home from the hospital, so I obliged. I decided to go about my normal routine with the boys in the morning and visit with Josh once Nathan went down for a nap.

I couldn't wait to see Josh and find out how he was holding up. I could not walk through the hospital hall fast enough. I rushed to the 14th floor to find him sitting up and having his vitals taken. His fever had come down. His blood pressure, which had gotten low, was starting to go up, but being monitored. It was a relief to see that Josh was ok physically. I wanted to cheer him up, so I got out a card from a dear saint from our church and began to read her card aloud to him. Before I finished reading the card, Josh had gone fast asleep. Drowsiness continued all afternoon. The blood pressure machine would go on automatically to check Josh's blood pressure, and he would not even awake. Josh is a light sleeper, so it was a surprise to see him sleep like this. He hasn't had much sleep during his hospital stay, so I'm thankful to see the goodness of God to let him sleep that well.

Eventually, she had to wake Josh up for a nasal sample to make sure he is not sick. It tuned out negative for influenza, but they are still checking for the common cold. They ordered Josh a smoothie the night before he couldn't keep food down. He tolerated a smoothie in the morning pretty well. During the time Josh was awake, his good friend Jason got to come in briefly to visit. Josh said that was therapeutic to him. Toward the end, his eyes were getting heavy, even though he had been in bed all day. We all decided to do a couple of laps around the unit. I'm so proud of Josh—he worked himself to doing a mile! While moving around is good for him, it also takes a lot out of him. It's all a balancing act—deciding the lesser of two evils. It reminds us of how much we all depend on God, and how ultimately the cure for all disease, sickness, and pain is found only through the eating of the tree of life granted only by faith in Christ who made a way for us to be reconciled to the Father. We're so glad that one day all who believe in Him will be granted access to the tree of life once more, to live eternally and never die again.

God truly did a miracle in sustaining and recovering Josh today. Thank you Lord! The doctors decided to administer the chemo trough Josh's IV slower, hoping that he will have a better night tonight. It seems Josh's symptoms get worst at night, so we need all the night owls praying throughout the night!

As hard as chemo, bone marrow transplantation, and hospital stays were, we indeed saw God use all of it for His glory. Josh was faithful in evangelism and prayer. Instead of being consumed with his own needs and pain, he reached out to care for other's spiritual needs. The Lord was kind to also send saints to minister to us as well. A particular man named Peter who had served as a missionary ran into Josh while his wife was in the unit. His wife had stage four cancer. They knew her time was short too. Peter was a slender older man with hair white as snow. He was friendly and strong in his Christian faith. The couple had served as missionaries' involved in strengthening pastors and leaders. That is exactly what Peter did in the hospital setting to encourage us even as his wife fought for life too. Whenever he would visit his wife, he would also stop to see Josh and offer spiritual refreshment and prayer. I was in the room on occasion and remember being somewhat upset one time he prayed surrendering Josh's life to the Lord. It was good preparation for what would follow. Pastor Peter acknowledged that death is far greater if that's what God willed. It was puzzling to me that a pastor would pray for the death of another, and one that young.

March 15, 2017

The countdown until Josh's bone marrow transplant is winding down. The day is quickly approaching. Friday, March 17th, Josh will receive new bone marrow from an unrelated donor. The Lord has been very kind in his provisions, love, and needed support through his people. The suffering is raw. It's something that Josh is enduring with much grace. Our entire family is experiencing pain in different ways. This is the most challenging circumstance we have ever been called to bear. Pray especially for our children throughout this trial, that they would know that God is good and loves them, that they would love Jesus more than ever.

Josh's new missionary and pastor friend Peter visited us and blessed us with the reading of Scripture and prayer. Refreshingly, today Josh did better–his temperature and blood pressure were normal and he hasn't needed oxygen again. We got to walk around the unit hand-by-hand many times, laughed together, cried together, and even got to pray for another couple going through similar circumstances with a father of a 4-year-old daughter having a transplant soon. We hope to have been used to plant seeds for salvation and that we form a relationship with them for the next couple of weeks. It's almost an instant bond to share in the same sufferings.

In a like manner, is our relationship with Christ. He suffered so much more, and he did nothing to deserve it. When we suffer for our obedience to His will, we experience some of what Jesus did on the cross. Often we suffer the consequences over sin. However, Jesus never sinned, yet suffered over our sins! When we endure watching others we love suffer, so does God as he watches all the pain and death that was caused by the fall. Thankfully, it doesn't end there. Our bond with Christ takes us into a beautiful eternal destination, a place where pain and sin and death is no more, and where we will share in his joy forever.

I enjoy keeping Josh company and being at his side, even in a dreary hospital ward. I hope that I will stay well enough to visit him daily. I'm thankful for the time I get to be with my beloved. Also tomorrow morning, March 16th, Josh will be undergoing a mild treatment of radiation. Even though his chemo is now over, he may still experience some more symptoms including his hair falling out. We were encouraged to find our Josh will be able to receive massage therapy from his hospital room to allevi-ate some of his symptoms. Please pray for both the radia-tion and the effects of the chemo. At the same time, pray that Josh would be encouraged and have faith that God can use even some gnarly drugs to bring about a wonder-ful cure and grant him more years of life to come. We take comfort in knowing God is present, that He abundantly loves and watches over us, and is powerfully answering prayers for Josh according to His good and perfect will.

Some days Josh did very well. Others he felt miserable. Either way, he pushed through and was always ready to share Christ. Our journey was much like what the hospital staff described—a series of ups and downs and unknowns at every corner. We knew at any given moment things would take a turn for the worst. I tried not to dwell on the "what-ifs" and held on to my faith that God could powerfully heal Josh. In the back of my mind, I knew the like-lihood of complications was high. However, I kept myself from thinking in the negative realm. I remained hopeful till the end.

March 16, 2017

The roller-coaster ride we are on has all of the fear without any of the fun. It's more like one of those rides you won-der why you ever got on, and wish there was some way to get off–only it's too late. You either endure or else you plunge out of your safety seat to your immediate death. I think this would be a way to describe how Josh feels right about now. The only difference is that Josh did not have much of choice. He didn't sign up for this because he thought he might get a thrill out of it. He only did this because to do otherwise would mean his bone marrow would quickly deteriorate beyond repair, and he would have surely died of this disease shortly.

The choice Josh made was to undergo a risky bone marrow transplant rather than to die without an intense fight. It was his only real chance of surviving at least a couple of years longer. With no real lasting cure for his disease, Josh knew his time on this planet was running thin. Over the four years we were married he learned to love as Christ loved, sacrificially even when it was painfully hard. In his last effort to live, my beloved did so out of love for his family and his church. He knew it would be excruciatingly painful.

Josh received a bone marrow transplant on March 17th, on Noah's birthday. It was not our choice. The medical team had done all they could to schedule the transplant as soon as possible, and it landed on that day. Noah had been sad about this. He expressed his grief in anger from the onset. His response was, "I don't' want my dad to die on my birthday." The doctors said that patient was not likely to die on the transplant day, so we assured Noah.

Nonetheless, the fear of Josh's death loomed over us like a dark cloud. Josh and I strived to see the sunshine hidden behind the gloom. We tried our best to ride the storm out. I hoped it would soon be all over, and life would go back to normal.

Josh and Papa took Noah to an Oregon Ducks game to celebrate his birthday ahead of time. One of the doctors suggested we look at it like a second birthday with new life for Josh. In that way, Noah would share birthdays with Josh. It gave us hope. The pastor of our church in Clackamas was teaching through the book of John. The week of Josh's transplant the pastor taught on chapter three, which speaks of a believer's new birth. I thought about how as Christians we are born again by the Spirit's regeneration and hoped for a type of physical new birth for Josh's failing bone marrow. I tried to muster up joy in our family's hearts by celebrating the transplant like it was a birthday. Josh was not convinced. Part of him knew the Lord would call him home to an even grander kind of rebirth in heaven. The day of Josh's transplant, I walked into his room with a gift and a birthday card. On the outside I put on a smile; inside my anxious heart was racing. Would this transplant give his body a physical rebirth and add years to his life?

The night before, I had gone shopping late after going home from the hospital to put the kids to bed. It would be Noah's birthday in a few hours, and I had no gift for him yet. Being physically and emotionally spent, I went to one of the few stores open late. I searched the toy rack for anything he might remotely enjoy. It could have been the worst birthday of Noah's life, yet our church family made it special for him. He got dozens of cards and packages from our church family back in Merlin. We also had visiting friends from our previous church visiting Arizona. They took Noah to a museum and restaurant for his birthday. Their presence and support meant so much to him and our entire family. The transplant went well that day, and we were at peace.

March 17, 2017

Today Josh received his new bone marrow. It was surprisingly an anti-climactic event. It was thankfully not very exciting. There weren't any significant complications. Josh's blood pressure was a bit off, but the doctors said it was an expected effect of getting the infusion. The medical team anticipated allergic reactions, so they gave him Benadryl beforehand and also slowed the infusion so that his body wouldn't react. We are hoping the Benadryl will help Josh sleep better tonight without the awful side effects of nightmares from taking sleeping pills. The transplant should take ten hours to go into Josh's bloodstream entirely.

Now, all we do is wait and pray that the two systems would work together to kill Josh's disease, then colonize the new system. The major risks come in the upcoming days and months ahead: Graft Versus Host Disease (GVHD) and infections which Josh is too weak to fight off. Until Josh's new system begins to reign in his body and does away with the old, he will have little to no immune system. So, we pray that God would protect Josh from any infections that could attack him. The other thing we pray for is that there would be only a small amount of GVHD to extinguish his old system of cells, yet not too much that it would damage his organs or end up taking his life.

Our good friend, Jason, likened Josh's bone marrow transplant to our need to do away with the old man to make room for the new. The old man functions in the flesh, but the new man created in the likeness of Jesus through faith in Him lives by his Spirit. However, to make room for the new, the old must be done away.

Jason and Becky took the boys to a fun bounce house place with their young kids. Then they took us all out for dinner to celebrate Noah's birthday and bought him a new Lego set, which he loved!

We had about a dozen or so friends mail Noah birthday cards and gifts. More are on their way. We also had the family pastor from our church here take Noah out for ice cream this morning. Noah was overwhelmed by how much he is loved. I reminded him that he is much loved by God first, then the outpouring of that is seen through others. God's love is inexhaustible!

All of your love, financial support and your deep concern for us is humbling. The prayers mean so much to us during a time when all we can do is hold on tight to our faith in a sovereign God who hears from heaven the prayers of his children, and answers in his perfect wisdom and time. We have seen God's love displayed brightly through His people. Many prayed at noon as Josh started his bone marrow transplant. It is only the beginning of our journey through a very dark valley, but in the end, we trust it will be all worth it.

Noah turned eleven years while Josh was at the hospital. It was a time of many changes in his life and a highly stressful time. He was going through physical changes and growth as a young man. Meanwhile, his hero and spiritual rock had a procedure that could end his life at any moment. We tried to booster Noah's faith in the procedure to some degree; however, we could not assure either of our children that they would see Daddy again. We all had to take it day by day.

March 20, 2017

Today I found Josh doing much better emotionally, even though he still feels lousy physically. He said, "I still don't feel good, but God has been very kind to me." His nurse today was a familiar one. Josh had the opportunity to have a long theological conversation with her and tell her about our hope in Christ. She said she enjoyed talking about philosophical things. In her efforts to cheer Josh up today, she felt compelled to pray for him even though she is not religious. She noticed that when Josh can minister to others, it helps lift his spirit. Moreover, she wanted to help Josh by letting him help her.

Interestingly, yesterday at church the pastor here in Clackamas taught on John, chapter four, where Jesus is vulnerable and thirsty, so he asks the Samaritan women for a drink, only to later give her living water unto eternal life. The pastor mentioned how sometimes we need to be vulnerable to gain inroads into sharing the good news of Jesus with others. In a way, that is what God is doing through Josh's weakest hours in the hospital. It's been good to get to build relationships with different nurses, especially if we get them again. Please pray for the salvation of those around us.

Another highlight for Josh today was getting a visit from a local man named Doug, whom we met through an old friend from LA. He felt led to visit Josh and uplifted his weary heart. He read some Scripture aloud, then read from their favorite—Jonathan Edwards. Josh said, "Doug had an excellent bedside manner." For the most part, he has not felt well enough to accept visitors. However, he needs encouragement from time to time.

Josh walked five laps and ate some oats, a cup of chicken noodle soup, apples with peanut butter, and some pudding. His white blood cells counts are at the zero point, so please pray for him to stay healthy enough for his body to regain strength.

The kids are doing ok. Nathan seems to be fighting a cold. His nose was a bit runny—clear mucus only, but then it cleared up. The kids have not been doing visits with Josh anymore, to play it safe. Please pray for them, as they deal with the emotional toll of not being able to see Daddy and vice-versa. Noah gets upset at times that he can't see Josh, and Nathan just doesn't understand. Today, the little guy asked where Daddy was. I told him Daddy was in the hospital, and he said, "No, he's not!" So I ended up showing him some pictures from a few days ago. He spends a long time looking through the photos, then seemed satisfied. We are working on trying to FaceTime again soon. Each of us is, at some level, experiencing loss. Josh feels like he's lost his way of life, and exchanged it for one of suffering and isolation. I feel like I have, in some capacity, lost my husband. Most times I don't give it much thought. Other times, it doesn't take much for me to break emotionally. The other day while driving alone, I got lost in town, and someone on the street yelled at me when I slowed down—I lost my composure and just started to sob. The kids must feel the same way. It's an arduous trial we are enduring. Your prayers, love, and encouragement are much appreciated!

Our time with Josh at the hospital was the hardest time of our life, yet also a season where we saw God's hand of compassion and mercy. It was a time of humbling and intense dependence on the Lord. Although I wanted to lie on the floor and cry my heart out, I had to stand with my head tall and steer our ship forward. Otherwise, we'd all fall apart. Tears could not escape my eyes around the children or in front of other people. It felt like the children and even to some extent, the church, was looking to me as their example. By God's grace, the strength to press on was supplied to me for that trying hour. At times, I interpreted a small answer to prayer as a sign of a larger answer for Josh's healing. The little answers to prayer were not in vain. They were my Father's loving arms of strength for that day to keep our head above the waves that came crashing against us.

March 25, 2017

The day flew by so fast for all of us, including Josh. He is bearing well living at the hospital. He doesn't necessarily have a routine. Things are always in consonant flux. However, he is learning to cope with his symptoms, discomfort, and a new environment. Josh has also been feeling better lately. He walked more than two miles today. Woohoo! Praise God!

It's also been great sharing laughs with him now that he has his sense of humor back. We even got to enjoy watching part of a movie together–Inn of the 6th Happiness. It's an old movie about a missionary in China, Gladys Aylward, who during wartime determinedly loved and helped orphans who were so vastly different than her. I am eager to return to be by Josh's side and finish the movie.

We talked to the transplant doctor who told us he is doing very well. He is expected to lose some of his hair soon, from the chemo. I asked what to expect from GVHD issues of in-compatibility. She told us usually people don't have GVHD quite this early on because new cells still haven't grown yet. The doctors say they want some GVHD to take place to kill off any remaining "bad" cells, yet not enough that it damages his organs. Since Josh has Fanconi Anemia (FA), he doesn't tolerate chemo. They had to give him very little chemo and radiation. They are hoping to control the GVHD to essentially cure him while not letting it kill him at the same time. We know that God is all-powerful and able to heal Josh, despite all of the danger, and that he can use the doctors to accomplish this if He wills. Josh says he is encouraged to persevere by thinking of our family and all that he wants to do in the future with the church and missions for the Lord.

Please pray for Josh to endure faithfully. Also, pray for Noah, Nathan, Katelynn and me–that we will all not grow faint nor despair, but grow in our Hope according to Romans 5:3-5, "Not only that, but we rejoice in our sufferings, knowing that suffering produces endurance, and endurance produces character, and character produces hope, and hope does not put us to shame, because God's love has been poured into our hearts through the Holy Spirit who has been given to us."

An Early Morning Conversation

What hour did you awake my love?
"Early enough to greet the LORD…"
But the sun has not yet warmed the earth
"Ah, but I was hungry for His word"

Was it on bended knee you begged Him come,
Tell me dear, did He meet you there?
"Ahe, to be sure He did, and as I knelt
I did consult my LORD in prayer"

And was He attentive to your voice
As its sweet tones broke the silence around
"Ahe He did indeed lend me His ears
And as I sought Him, He was found"

Your faithfulness to Him is great my dear
For you renew it every morning
"Ah, but tis the faithfulness that He imparts
That enables all of my imploring"

Copyright Josh "J.D." Seibert 2012

[Chapter 8]

Pressing On in the Trenches

S uffering strengthened our faith and produced hope in the unseen spiritual benefits it brings. God used us in the lives of those around us, which helped give us the motivation to press on. With our eyes on our mission to win others to Christ, it made the battlefield easier to carry on. There were times when we felt wounded too deep to move a muscle. Then, God faithfully showed us that in our suffering we were to make His name known, and that we were not alone. Every time we shared Christ with another patient or family member, God rejuvenated us. He gave us fuel for our engines to keep pressing forward in the race.

March 26, 2017

Today Josh got his last dose of a drug that prevents GVHD—it's a low dose type of chemo. He doesn't usually have a problem with this one, yet has an allergic reaction to the white blood cell infusions. He had a rash on his body, so they decided not to give him any white cells today. We are still waiting and praying for his bone marrow cells engraft well. As far as energy is concerned, Josh is doing considerably well. He walked another two miles. He says his goal is to walk one before I arrive, then walk another one together.

When I got to the hospital after lunch, Josh was already napping. I waited for him in the lounge. As I was surfing the net, one of the other patients, a 30-year old man named Zach, came in. I had seen him a few times before, usually accompanied by a worker from the hospital talking about wanting to smoke a cigarette. The patients on the unit are not allowed to smoke. Plus, it's an indoor unit with strict sanitary precautions. In the two weeks that Josh has been there, they've only allowed him to go onto another floor once, and that was to receive radiation. Zach remarked how he usually sees me on the treadmill. I told him I wasn't on the treadmill because I was wearing heels since coming directly from church. He commented that he wished he could go to church. I told him my husband was a pastor and could visit him if he'd like. He said he would appreciate that and needed prayer. Then, he invited his nurse Rachel and me to play a game of bowling with him on the Wii Fit in the lounge. We both agreed. They beat me, but it was still a joy to see Zach have fun. It was an even greater joy to see Zach receive the healing balm of the gospel later when Josh joined us. Josh got to pray for him, then he asked for prayer for his mother and brothers that are grieving him. So Josh prayed some more. Then Zach wanted to pray for Josh! His prayer was one of humility, and it brought a tear to our eyes. He acknowledges that he had fallen away from walking with the Lord and wants to be restored. Please keep Zach in your prayers!

Josh is making friends, blessing others including myself with his sense of humor and love. Time is passing by quicker. This is such an answer to prayer, as he was in agony when time seemed to go by slowly. We got to finish the rest of the movie Inn of the 6th Happiness—it was a great movie, even though I later learned it wasn't as accurate as it could have been. Nonetheless, it was an inspiring story of faith through Christ and courage, despite incredible difficulties and suffering.

Josh was such an inspiration to all. Amidst the deepest thorn in his flesh, he looked not for his own relief for that of others. His deepest concern was to share Christ and pray for others. Before entering the hospital doors, he determined it in his mind. When we were weary and questions flooded our minds, the resolve was challenging. We were thankful for the believers that had gone before us in similar circumstances and those He had cross our path to encourage us. For example, one of the social workers, a Christian, prayed with me at the most critical moments. I also read a book by Dave Furman called *Being There* on how to be a loving and helpful caregiver to my husband. Words like this ministered to my grieving heart, "Compassionate caretaker, do you think he will abandon you now in the midst of your own genuine loss? No, he won't. Rest assured that because of Jesus, there is always hope, even in the darkest moments of your life." (Furman, 29).

Josh was stirred by the Spirit and other saints to endure everything for the sake of the elect. (2 Tim2:10). One particular friend from his college days, Adam Holland, spoke to him over the phone and encouraged him from a book he wrote about his journey with cancer. "In my trial of brain cancer, I had the great delight to see someone come to Christ in salvation through God's work in my life. Through my story the Lord led one of His precious children to Him in faith. When I heard this I realized that my cancer was worth it, and I would do it all over again if it meant that just one person would come to salvation." (Holland, 19) Another man who heavily influenced Josh was John Piper. Although, he didn't know Piper personally, he knew him through his books. John Piper's *Don't Waste Your Cancer* and *Suffering and the Sovereignty of God* inspired him too.

As a result, Josh then wrote and prepared cancer tracts to pass out at the hospital. They were simple but profound. Josh printed at least two hundred of these tracts and passed out half. He prayerfully gave them out or left them in strategic places like hospital waiting rooms. On the cover of the 5x6 card was a picture of a doctor holding a blackboard with the word "Cancer." The other side read:

> Nothing is perhaps more earth-shattering to us than to hear our doctors say one word: cancer! The mere word awakens all kinds of unanswered questions, leaving us feeling blindsided and scared. What will happen to my loved ones and me? What kind of treatment will I go through? Is there a cure? Cancer forces us to answer questions we hoped we would never have to ask. But there are some questions that physicians can't answer. Questions that can only be answered by "The Great Physician," Jesus. The Bible tells us that God sent Jesus to heal us of the cancer of sin by becoming our blood donor that we might have eternal life by repenting and believing. God has provided a perfect match in Jesus that we might be transfused with His precious blood and cured of the cancer of sin. Ephesians 1:7 says "In Jesus we have redemption through his blood, the forgiveness of our sins, according to the riches of his grace." Jesus is the ultimate cure for our cancer. Will you turn to the Great Physician of your soul for healing, strength and comfort during this difficult time?

Josh found much joy from being able to minister to others at the hospital and share the wonderful news of the gospel to those dying to hear good news. He had a natural way of gaining the trust of others. Josh could make the saddest stranger smile and become a friend. His sense of humor opened doors to conversations with virtually anyone. The young dying man named Zach became fond of him. Zach ended up wanting to follow Christ too thanks to Josh's example. "Our response to pain and suffering can be a powerful witness to the watching world." (Furman, 100) Josh asked how he could pray for those he met and genuinely cared for their souls. He still saw himself as a pastor and evangelist even while away from his church. The staff granted him that freedom since they knew he was a pastor. He couldn't wait to get back to serve the church he longed to see again.

March 27, 2017

This morning, we had the delight of having visitors—our dear church friends and ministry partners, Dwight and Elaine. They had a nice visit with Josh and brought a big smile to his face. Afterward, Katelynn and the boys met us by the tram station to wave to Daddy again. Nathan had been talking about wanting to do it again. He was so excited to see Daddy through his room window and enthusiastic to ride the tram. We took the scenic sky tram to a burger place named Little Big Burger, where we got little half-sized burgers with a fat patty and an extra helping of fries. Nathan loved it and devoured every last bite. Noah, on the other hand, was disappointed that the burgers were so little. Something we are all trying to learn is to be thankful even during the disappointments in life. God indeed gives us so much through his grace and mercy. At times we can forget to count our blessings in life, and we miss out on seeing His love and goodness.

Today, Josh was blessed to be able to do a Bible study with Zach on John chapter three, and the new birth. Zach genuinely wanted to study the Bible with him, and it energized Josh to be able to minister to someone in such need. Zach's cancer is much more advanced. He may not make it. The doctors aren't sure what they can do for him. He can still experience full healing and life eternal no matter what the outcome in this short life. Josh thinks

Zach is now in a right place spiritually. Please continue to pray for him. He is likely to get discharged tomorrow.

Josh's doctor delivered more good news this morning, telling us his numbers are already starting to rise. They went from below zero to one. It is earlier than expected! However, along with his numbers picking up comes the risk for GVHD. Please pray that God, our creator, would sovereignly direct all of this happening in his body to give Josh complete healing. Regardless of what may come our way next, pray for us to rest in his infinite wisdom and perfect will.

It was both a privilege and agony to come alongside my husband for such a risky treatment. Some days we were full of hope. Others seemed hopeless. No matter what the outcome, my husband assured me it would be all for our good and God's glory. I believed him with all my heart. Over the four years of being married, we got to the point of intimate trust. The doubts and fears that arose soon dissipated. I watched my Christian soldier march on with courage, and had no option but to follow suit close behind him. It was a blessing to go through the trial together while being uplifted by the prayers of the saints around us. Sometimes our grasp for faith was a real struggle. Not long after, we would feel carried on the wings of prayers. This was a poem Josh wrote while in the hospital that encouraged his heart and those around him.

Mooring of a Traveling Soul

God of all strength, God of all Might

You hold us fast and we hold tight

You never give up on any one of our souls

In the great tempest of life, you're still in control

Cause you're the unchanging God, in an ever-changing world

You are the fountain of youth,

Our very lives you restore

You are the anchor of our souls and the steadfast riggings of our hearts,

Jesus, you are the moorings of my soul

Copyright Josh "J.D." Seibert 2017

The Lord felt nearer to us than ever before in that raging storm. No matter where the wind blew, our anchor held tightly to our Savior. Our faith could not have survived the testing without His grace. We had to constantly and desperately rely on Him for wisdom and strength for every hour. Josh was an excellent example to me of suffering to the glory of God. In his pain, he chose not to focus on himself, but on Christ and those around him. He was always ready to give a defense of his faith and fought for the perishing unsaved souls all around us. Moreover, because of Josh's saving faith in Christ, he was ready to meet Him. The worst possible outcome of death could only be the best possible outcome for him in heaven.

March 29, 2017

Today Josh felt a bit worse than yesterday and still had the same cold. They started giving him shots in his tummy that helps produce white blood cells. Once his body produces white blood cells, they'll fight off his cold. Lord willing, in a few more days his white blood count will go up, and he can come home. As his white blood count goes up, so does his immunity. While this is a good thing, it also means that he will be at higher risk for GVHD since his body may likely want to fight off his new foreign bone marrow cells.

We had a long conversation with Josh's nurse. He is a bright guy and quite humorous. We were glad to share our faith in the one true God revealed in the Bible–among other things like the principle of right and wrong, the binary nature of our belief, and whether or not the heart of a man is inherently good. Josh and I went into some apologetics with him. It was a friendly and peaceful debate, spontaneously started while he was on his way out of Josh's room. He stood by the door literally about to exit the room—for 40 minutes!

It goes to show we must be ready anytime to give a defense for the hope that is in us. Please continue to pray not only for Josh and the other patients here but for the friendly staff here as well. It can be discouraging when people don't embrace the life-giving truth. Still, it is a relief to know that regeneration is not up to us. Psalm 139 brings me comfort, knowing that even before a word is on my month, God knew it. During trials like this, I am so thankful for a solid foundation of knowing God is sovereign over even these small details in our life as well as the big events like how many days we live on this earth.

It is still a challenge every day to put that knowledge into practice by living out my faith and love for my Lord without fear or reservations. I too say, "Lord, I believe, help my unbelief. (Mark 9:24.) Since Josh has been isolated in his room now, he hasn't been able to see anyone else on the unit other than the staff that comes into his room plus me. Earlier, an art teacher was able to bring some canvas cards and color pencils. Josh made fun cards for the boys. His nurse said that Josh is likely to have this cold only for another week and by then it may be time to discharge him.

Josh caught a cold. Some told us this simple bug could result in pneumonia and lead to his death. Despite, the persistent cold, Josh's numbers seemed to be doing outstanding. His body received the bone marrow without any significant complications. The biggest concern from the doctors in letting Josh leave the hospital was the risk for GVHD. Josh was anxious to be released from the hospital. He felt like a caged bird. The longer Josh stayed in isolation because of his cold, the more depressed he became. Josh thrived being around people. He did everything his nurses and doctors told him to in hopes of being let home early. Josh's blood counts were high enough that he got discharged after only three weeks of hospitalization instead of four. We were overjoyed to spend our Easter together at our little home away from home in Portland.

March 31, 2017

Today Josh was discharged from the hospital! His counts were at 570 so they let him go this evening. We had a beautiful day filled with sunshine and joyful beginnings. Josh got to sleep in his bed and hopefully will get uninterrupted sleep. The kids were ecstatic to see Josh. Nathan's expression when he saw Daddy at the door was precious. For a moment it looked like he couldn't believe his eyes, then he jumped out of his chair and ran to him. Noah walked in from helping friends with some yard work with a big smile on his face. He had to sanitize thoroughly before greeting Daddy. We were all happy to have Josh back with us! We also had to be cautious about the possible risks of infections and such. Please pray our family would learn new routines and precautions quickly, and for continued recovery for Josh without infections or GVHD.

God, in His abundant grace, gave us a couple of weeks with Josh back at our Portland home before having to say goodbye. The boys didn't have much interaction with him at the hospital. It served as preparation for a longer absence. We did not know how soon Josh could be leaving us again. In some ways, we anticipated the likelihood of rushing him back to the emergency room. Our hearts were being prepared, but could not bear to fully accept its weight. We never fully understood what was going on. In all of this, we rested in God's all-knowing character and sovereign rule in all the affairs of His children.

April 3, 2017

Having Josh at home is such a sweet blessing. I'm glad to have my shepherd back and for the kids to have their rock again! We are delighted to be able to enjoy simple things with him like sitting in the living room while playing a board game, or going outside for a walk together. We've been walking every day—rain or shine. Today we had the delight of another beautiful sunny day in Portland with a high of 60. Thank you, God!

Spring is in the air, and all kinds of gorgeous flowers and trees are blooming all around us. Our favorites are cherry blossoms. There are still more trees and flowers ready to bloom. We anticipate the roses blooming in the upcoming months.

Josh has started to bloom as well. Over the weekend his counts increased dramatically. His neutrophils went from about 570 to 3,000 in just the last few days. 3,000 is actually in the normal range. Although, he still feels very fatigued. His platelets have been down, and the doctors were expecting to give him a transfusion. Overnight they increased instead of decreasing as predicted, so he didn't need a transfusion after all. It's not uncommon to need another one shortly. Another reason to thank the Lord is for Josh not experiencing any GVHD. Praise the Lord—

who hears our supplications. Therefore, please keep praying. We anticipate Josh fully blooming with his new ideal donor cells in the upcoming months. That is our prayer.

God was present in every crazy turn of our journey through the valley of the shadow of death. We could not see the sinking hole in front of us. Meanwhile, God was able to see it clearly and brace us for the shock. When we were discouraged, God comforted our hearts with the little desires of our hearts. One afternoon, Josh asked me to drive him around town to get out of the house. We didn't have a particular destination. Josh told me which way to go in search for a spot near one of the rivers that runs through Portland to scope it out for future fishing. We almost gave up. I asked if I should check around the corner and proceeded. Even though it was a busy city area, just around the other side, we found a little secluded opening to a small river. It was drizzling. Nonetheless, we put on our hoodies and went out for a short walk in the rain. Josh was so thankful and happy to have found the place. He was hopping on the rocks as I pled him to be careful. He was like a kid at Disneyland. Josh was so excited and kept praising God for our adventure. The outing was a sweet refreshment to our soul. We held hands and thanked God for His kindness.

April 17, 2017

Josh is halfway to Day 60 when he will be able to regain some of his freedom. He'll get to go out in public (during less busy hours) and eat out again! It has been a bit of stormy voyage thus far, yet our captain and master, Jesus Christ, sustains us along the way. He gives us his Spirit to bring joy and peace even in the darkest nights.

It was a challenge having two sick kids with the flu at home. However, they are now on the mend. Amazingly, Josh did not get the flu. Praise the Lord! When Josh's nurse practitioner found out Noah was sick, she wanted the boys tested and put on an anti-virus medication. Even though we dislike having the kids on drugs, this is a serious enough threat to Josh where we have no choice. We pray the kids to tolerate the Tamiflu, and for them not to have any of the adverse reactions warned. Noah's flu has already been cut short by a couple of days, and Nathan's high fever broke almost the next day. Today, he still has a low-grade fever and was back to feeling crummy.

Katelynn has been an immense help. Nathan's fever reached 103.5, and we had to keep on top of his temperature as well as wiping everything down with non-toxic disinfecting wipes. We tried to keep the boys isolated. We all got to wear fun masks around the house too. There was no way to keep little Nathan separated anywhere or to keep a mask on him.

By Resurrection Sunday, the boys had been feeling better and even got to go outside in our yard on a warm sunny day to do an Easter egg hunt. We didn't go to church since the boy had just had fevers. Instead, we tried to watch the Grace Community Church Livestream service on my choppy cell phone. The kids enjoyed Easter crafts with Katelynn, their new Easter baskets, and gifts from Grandma Kim and Papa Don. We are so thankful to everyone who sent cards, texts, and encouraging messages to our little family. We are blessed and without a doubt beloved by God. We love you and appreciate your ongoing prayers.

The flu crept into our house despite our rigorous efforts to prevent it. We were frightened. First, we quarantined Noah in his room, then we tried to do the same with Nathan when he got it. Despite the illness and the anxiety of frequent doctor appointments and a rigid diet, I was determined to remain positive.

Josh was home! I mapped out our calendar for the next two years, counting his post-transplant days. I knew the exact date when he would be able to eat out again. He was counting down the days until he could go to church or a social setting like a grocery store. He was not allowed to go to any public places. We both longed for life to go back to some degree of normalcy again. Our earnest plea to the Lord was for healing and our life restored. Easter was a lovely time of celebrating the spiritual life that kept our hearts and minds in Christ. We relished the sweetest of hope for new life.

Daily Petition

In thy footsteps wilt I trace

Lead me daily in thy grace

Grant unto me life anew

And let my portion be solely you

Direct my steps along thy path

And let me not provoke thy wrath

Give thy spirit to instill

And lead me in thy perfect will

For though my sins have been grave

Though hast sought my soul to save

Incline my heart to obey

And consider my petition when I pray

Let thee alone be what satisfies

Let no earthly form catch my eyes

Take up and dwell in my abode

Carry my burden and my load

Continue your good work in me
Till all concludes in eternity
Chasten my thought, action, and deed
And let me help those in need

Copyright "J.D." Seibert 2008

[Chapter 9]

Unexpected Twists and Turns

S pringtime started to peek through the Portland landscape. However, the chill of winter was still upon us, and various illnesses were still going around. Josh began to have problems with his throat, but didn't think much of it. He initially thought it was the lingering cold he had throughout. Even before being admitted into the hospital, he had the virus prior to the transplant. The cold never went away. We worried his cold might morph into something worse. It was the last thing he needed to add to his critical state.

A stubborn fever coupled with swelling drove him to be admitted into the hospital voluntarily. When Josh went in, the doctors thought it might only be a minor complication. The boys said goodbye to Daddy thinking they'd see him again in a few days. We all thought the hospital trip would be short-lived, and we'd return to our new routines of caring for him at home. We had gone to the emergency room the night before, and they ended up sending us back home the same night. The next day Josh saw his doctor, and she didn't think he needed to stay in the hospital. Later that same night, his fever and throat pain continued to increase. He got admitted to OHSU as a mere precautionary measure.

April 22, 2017

Josh was admitted back into the hospital last night for a persistent fever. It started as a low-grade fever on Thursday night and continued to progress. It has been hard to try to determine the cause since he had not only fevers and chills but also cold-like symptoms, a small amount of GVHD, plus his lymph nodes on his throat are swelling. We spent most of yesterday at the clinic, and half the night in the ER. At the ER, they gave Josh antibiotics and sent him home. At the clinic, they tried to come up with an out-patient plan to address Josh's symptoms so he wouldn't need to go to the hospital. Josh's nurse instructed him to go home and call if his fever exceeded 101. Josh asked if she could take his temperature right then at the clinic. His temperature was 101.5, so she gave him Tylenol and started him on antibiotics, but still sent him home. About two hours after being at home, Josh's fever came back up to over 101 despite the fever-reducer. After talking to our nurse and going back and forth, we decided to have him admitted.

A CT scan on his throat show clues to the type of infection Josh may have. They found liquid and signs of a bacterial infection. They are hoping the antibiotics will stop the possible infection early enough that they would not need to cut him open and drain it through surgery. It would be too early post-transplant to remove the fluid through an operation, even if they wanted to. They were surprised that Josh came back with signs of a throat infection since Josh had not complained much of any symptoms other than the swollen lymph nodes, which everyone thought related to his cold. Josh has been trying to tough it out too. He mentioned sometime last week that he had a sore throat, but said it wasn't bad enough for me to call on it.

Today, they took a sample into the lab to test it for Strep. We are thankful to have some clues, but are waiting and praying for more answers. We pray that Josh will be able to fight whatever this is, with the aid of the antibiotics and, more importantly, the Lord's help! Our nurse today said she is confident that given his blood counts, he will be able to fight this off. We trust in God's sovereignty and purpose in all of this, yet the process remains scary. Please pray for Josh to get some much needed rest and comfort in the Lord during this trial-some time; and for wisdom for the doctors and medical team involved.

For the entire first week, the doctors thought Josh only had an infection. They placed him on antibiotics, and that was it. The doctors kept waiting for lab cultures to show an infection. They never did. There was no infection, and his condition worsened. The doctors could find no answers. They started to rule things out. It was not the flu. It was not an infection, which was common in his kind of transplant. It did not have anything to do with his cold. It was evident after a few days of no indication of any infection that the situation could be more complicated than the doctors initially thought.

April 24, 2017

The past couple of days have been tough. My heart breaks for how sick Josh has been. He has been spiking fevers even with fever reducer around the clock. With his temperatures, come chills and discomfort. Josh tells me the Lord is teaching him perseverance through this trial and that's so inspiring for me to hear. Still, it hurts to watch him go through the pain. The doctors have Josh on a general spectrum of antibiotics for the past four days. The antibiotics do not seem to help at all. Although they don't know the details at this point, they think it's a bacterial infection inside the right side of his throat. The medical team did a CT scan of his throat today and saw not much of a change. Josh says he feels about the same, only slightly worse. He seems more congested and having difficulty breathing. The next thing they are planning, if his infection continues not to improve, is to do what they call a "straightforward" surgery to drain out some of the fluid to take a sample to identify the type of infection. Surgery will allow them to target it with specific antibiotics.

The hospital moved Josh upstairs a level up to the BMT unit, where he had his transplant so the team can keep a better eye on him. The crazy thing is, they even moved him into the same room he had with the beautiful view of Portland by the sky tram. God shows his goodness to us in many ways like this to boost our faith. Humanly it still can be a challenge to find joy in the times of trouble. Nonetheless, we have experienced a kind of peace above understanding through the Holy Spirit who lives in us, because of the redemptive work of salvation through Jesus in our lives. We are ever thankful for Christ taking our place on the cross that we may not be punished for our sins but freely have eternal life. Please pray for this peace and joy to fill our souls and overflow to others. In the morning Josh's medical team will see how he's doing and decide whether or not they will do the surgery tomorrow. He got some sleep last night, and we hope he gets good sleep again tonight. Your prayers for tomorrow are much appreciated!

At the home front, Katelynn has done a fantastic job with the boys and has kept the boys busy. I have been absent more. I try to be there at the hospital when the doctors come and discuss updates and treatments options. This morning they asked Josh to stop drinking or eating because he may end up having surgery. It was not until four in the evening when they informed us that he wouldn't be having surgery until tomorrow. We understand things take longer at hospitals, but it's especially hard for Nathan to understand why mom needs to be gone all day. He naturally misses me. I am comforted that Nathan loves his nanny too.

For a momma bear to be away from her little cubs is heart-wrenching. My love for my husband compelled me to be there as his helpmate and advocate as much as I could. Meanwhile, my two-year-old missed seeing not only his daddy but also his mommy. It was easier for our oldest to comprehend why we were away, and he made some friends in the church. However, the kids were both on restrictions, especially when fighting colds. They were dealing with many emotions as they stayed at home waiting for news from me at the end of the day. During this time Noah dealt with guilt, fear, and anger. Nathan struggled with sorrow and was unable to comprehend what was happening. I wanted to stay by their side and assure them everything would be ok. However, I also needed care for Josh and didn't know what would take place from one day to the next. Even a procedure like surgery could be added to the schedule overnight.

April 26, 2017

The surgery went well yesterday. Josh woke up from the anesthesia and said, "That wasn't so bad!" He didn't feel sore. He had one of the best surgeons, and he didn't see any infection, which helped the doctors get a clearer picture of what's happening. Josh has tested positive for the Epstein Barr Virus (EBV). Also, they are doing a PET scan to make sure the EBV has not caused cancer in his lymph nodes. Since he is a bone marrow transplant patient with the EBV, he is at risk for a type of complication called Post-Transplant Lymphoproliferative Disease (PTLD) that's very aggressive. Our prayer is that he wouldn't have it. Ultimately though, we ask that God's will be done. He is sovereign over all of it.

The doctors want to start Josh right away on a drug called Rituximab to combat the EBV and get him feeling better quickly. He began his first dose tonight along with some steroids. The steroids will help prevent reactions to the drug plus help his swelling to go down. Josh is feeling miserable right now. His neck is enormous; his feet swollen; he's been running fevers almost non-stop even with Tylenol; and has constant chills. Josh's breathing is not normal, and his throat is sore. Despite the terrible suffering Josh is going through, he continues to be anchored by God and says this is all being used to define him.

The doctor said with the new medication his symptoms should start improving almost right away. The drug is a form of chemotherapy and could cause side effects or reactions, so please pray for this to go smoothly. Josh tends to have allergies and is sensitive to chemo. He was given Benadryl and steroids to help with possible reactions. Additionally, they will be administering the Rituximab extra slowly through his IV. Josh's doctors and medical team have been bringing different doctors together and agreed to call specialists on FA from Minnesota to be extra cautious.

We've had the opportunity to pray with a couple of people during this past week and to plant gospel seeds. One of the social workers here is a believer. She came to check on us while the nurses were taking Josh's vitals, and I asked her if she could pray for us. It was neat for her to pray for us aloud with others in the room. Josh said he was surprised she was allowed to do that with how uncomfortable some people get when Christians pray. Yesterday while Josh was in surgery, I went into the waiting room and got to pray with a lady for her dad. She was under much emotional toil because her elderly father was not breathing very well after the surgery. We've also been playing the ESV Audio Bible out loud for Josh, which has ministered to both of us. Plus, we never know who else may be listening.

People all around us watched as Josh held his peaceful demeanor and bold testimony for Christ. He sought to honor God with his last words. With all the unknowns, Josh's last expressed concern was to make sure we were still tithing while away. During one of our final conversations, he asked me to write the church a check. Then, he asked me what the doctors thought about his condition. I responded, "The only thing they know for sure is that you have Epstein Barr Virus (EPV), and might have something called PTDL. They say either should be treatable with the chemo they gave you." He responded, "I hope it's nothing worse."

I went out to a drug store to pick up an over-the-counter nasal solution a nurse recommended. When I returned, a young doctor was standing by his door while another doctor stood inside explaining to Josh that he needed to do down to the Intensive Care Unit. The young doctor outside informed me they needed to take him to a one-on-one unit—in case Josh stopped breathing.

The next thing I knew, the team was escorting him to the ICU. The Christian social worker who had prayed with us walked by my side every step down to the ICU where they put a breathing tube down Josh's throat. She took me aside so I wouldn't watch his agony while they inserted the tube. She explained how scary the ICU would be, the risks involved, then prayed with me. It was a sign that Josh's time might be drawing to a close. My heart couldn't resign to losing him. I held on to believe he would come out victorious.

April 27, 2017

Today has not brought the relief as we were hoping. Josh got his first dose of the Rituximab last night, and it did not improve things. The good news is they are pretty sure he doesn't have a bacterial infection, even from the surgery. The bad news is his swelling got worst and started closing his airway passage. The doctors don't know why the Rituximab did not provide any relief. The medical team decided to move Josh to the ICU because of the danger of his airway completely closing. They wanted to play it safe and keep a better eye on him at the ICU, where he will practically have a nurse to himself. They also decided to insert a breathing tube preemptively now, rather than wait when the airway gets tighter.

The past 3-4 days Josh has had CAT scans, PET scans, and surgery, causing eating restrictions. Now with the breathing tube, he can't eat at all. The doctors also put in a feeding tube. He's hooked up to all kinds of devices, making him extremely uncomfortable, so they are sedating him. He wakes up now and then, but he can't talk with the tubes in his mouth. He communicated through hand gestures though. When they were taking him to have the CAT scan he signaled with two hands together. Since they were pointed down, I thought he had to go to the bathroom, but he kept nodding his head as to say no. One of the nurses understood this signal earlier but had left the room. They went to find that nurse to ask her what the sign meant, and she said, "Pray." Bless Josh's heart! I got to pray aloud for Josh before he had his CAT scan done.

The different medical teams are trying to put their brains together and make sense out of what's going on. They highly suspect it to be Post-Transplant Lymphoproliferative Disease (PTLD) as a result of the Epstein Barr Virus (EBV) that they've confirmed has been increasing in his body. If it is PTLD, they are saying it's very aggressive, and his FA makes it challenging to treat with chemo. The doctors are pushing to get confirmation of PTLD tomorrow afternoon from pathology since it's an urgent need. They continue to run all kinds of tests to try to determine the root cause. It may have to do with Josh's genetic disease, which caused his MDS in the first place. FA increases the likelihood of cancers and tumors, and PTLD would be like a form of cancer. Adding to the difficulty, not all doctors, like the ICU team, know a whole lot about FA. I am thankful that Dr. Jewel is more familiar with in FA and is overseeing it.

Moreover, I'm thankful that God is overseeing all of this. It comforts me to know that God is the Great Physician, and he knows all things. In His book were written all of Josh's days, before there was even one.

The social worker came to talk to me and walk me through the process of moving Josh to the ICU. In God's kindness, she is also a believer and has been praying for us. I was able to cry with her away from Josh's presence so that he wouldn't worry about me. It's still so hard to watch Josh go through all of this. It's even harder for Josh going through all of this! Naturally, his anxiety level has increased, which also hasn't helped with his breathing trouble.

Please keep the children in your prayers. Josh's dad is flying out tomorrow morning to help with the boys and to be there with Josh. Our prayer is that Josh starts turning toward recovery and for him get to come home to us. Our hearts ache to see him suffer like this. Thank you for your friendship and partnership with us through prayer to our interceder Jesus Christ, from whom we have direct access to the throne of God! His will be done, his kingdom come.

While Josh was in the ICU, his life was hanging in the balance. He only had me, and I didn't have him to consult. I was alone for most of it. I had to lean on Christ and people He placed in our path. Perhaps I would have been overcome by a sea of depression if I did not have to steer the ship. My mind stayed set on survival mode. By God's grace, I was determined to make the best decisions for Josh. For that to happen, my emotions needed to be left at the foot of the cross. Those critical days, I spent all my waking hours at the hospital. I would go home to say goodnight to the boys, try to get some sleep and return early the next day before the sun came up. I wanted to be there before the doctors came to huddle around his room to discuss his treatment plan for the day. If I wasn't there, who would speak up for Josh while sedated? He only had me to advocate for him. The doctors often looked disappointed and at a loss for options. Although I trusted God's ability to pull Josh through, I also realized that might not be His plan. I wanted to honor the Lord and Josh's wishes more than anything.

August 28, 2017

Josh showed some improvement today. His swelling went down somewhat, and he's breathing on his own mostly. They still have the breathing tube in place because he's at risk of his airway closing. They did an ultrasound on him today. Preliminary results confirmed Josh has PTLD or a form of lymph node cancer, and it is likely an aggressive one. It has affected not only his throat but also in his armpits, his stomach, and possibly his brain. Dr. Jewell will come in to talk to us about our options in the morning. She has been caring and diligent to research the different drugs and their toxicity risk on FA patients. She even called one of the best FA specialists in Minnesota and will reach out to another one. Please pray for us to have wisdom in all the decisions—that we'd all be well informed, including the doctors. We want Josh to be a part of the decision making process. However, having a breathing tube down his throat makes it so he cannot talk.

I asked God if the doctors could take that breathing tube out ASAP. If the swelling in his throat would go down, they could remove it. It's almost unbearable for him. It's hard for him to communicate with us and that's frustrating to him. With his hands restrained, he won't yank the breathing tube out. Today he signaled that he was hungry and thirsty. He can't eat or drink. All the nurse could do was to clean his mouth to try to provide relief for his dry mouth. It reminded me of the suffering Jesus went through on the cross when he was thirsty, and they finally gave him wine mixed with gall to drink. I told Josh he reminds me of Christ and what Christ did for us on the cross. Pray for him to be comforted and ministered to by the Holy Spirit. Please pray for him to be alert when we talk to the doctor, and for all of us to have discernment and wisdom on how to proceed.

Josh was a strong example of suffering well. He lived and died well. He fought for his life, even when it hurt. He did so because he believed life was precious and only to taken by God himself. He also had faith in God's sovereignty. He knew God was ultimately in charge of all the hospital personnel and ordained the kiln of affliction in that particular hospital, at that specific time. We saw a glimpse of God's glorious purposes in the ways Josh got to minister to others. However, we may never know the full measure of the plans and accomplishments God brought forth from our journey.

April 29, 2017

Today Josh was getting pretty restless and anxious to get the breathing tube out—especially when they completely turned off his sedative drugs. He could feel everything. It's very uncomfortable—painful. It didn't help that he got lots of steroids too; they make people anxious. On top of that, they told him that they were about to take the tubes out, a couple of minutes before the doctor walked in to explain they would have to wait longer. He had his hopes up already.

On the bright side, Josh was very alert and cognitive even coming out of sedatives. The doctors had to bring him up to speed on what's going on, but it's normal to have amnesia at first. So basically, Josh is breathing on his own. He technically doesn't need a breathing tube. Right now, he's breathing fine, which makes it so tempting to get it off. Noah wanted to visit Josh, and he got to come with Papa today. It was hard for him to see Daddy like this though. Josh got to be awake while he visited, so that was special. Please keep praying for the kids!

It's an answer to prayer that they were able to explain Josh's options with us both. Even though Josh shed a tear and was not happy about it, he agreed to stay on the breathing tube to pursue further possible treatment. Josh is being a champ and fighting for his life! At this point, they're doing more of what they've already done with steroids and chemo targeting the EBV. Josh is getting another dose of the Rituximab tonight and waiting to see if he can get some T-cells as soon as possible. The Rituximab could make his neck swollen worse, which is why they chose to keep the breathing tube. While we wait for the T-cells, we may need to do an adjusted dose of another chemotherapy drug to keep him going long enough to get those T-cells and hopefully start that therapy as soon as possible.

Josh chose life. He chose to die to himself, that he might live. He hated the breathing tube. It was invasive and painful. He chose to leave it jammed into his agitated throat. He could have thrown in the towel. It would have been easier to ask to get the tube out and allow himself the possibility of suffocating from a closed airway. Josh knew the glories of heaven awaited him. He also knew his health had taken a turn for the worse. He practiced what he preached in a sanctity of life message entitled, "From the Womb to the Tomb."

April 30, 2017

Josh has been moving very much today while in the ICU. It was alarming to me to come this morning at 6:00 a.m. to find that Josh had unconsciously yanked his feeding tube off of his nose. It is a natural reaction to want to pull it out. He had attempted to do so before. Since then, he has been calm, but he's needed more sedation. When Josh's doctor came in to talk to us, they took his sedation down somewhat, but Josh was unable to wake up and respond. He was restless and uncomfortable. The doctor did not have any decisions for him to make yet, so we spared Josh any more pain, and turn back up his sedatives. The plan, for now, is to try and get the tube out tomorrow if his swelling does not get worse. The doctor doesn't think it should.

Then by Tuesday, we should find out whether or not we will have the T-cells and when. We hope for T-cells to start mild chemo. Dr. Jewel got consensus from FA doctors all over the country that a mild dose is the best thing! Please pray for the successful treatment of his PTLD.

The hardest thing for us as a family has been watching Josh suffer. Noah was brave to come to see him yesterday, but he doesn't want to see him like this again. He asks when he will be out and home with us again. That is our longing—to see Josh back home with us soon!

I've tried playing the audio Bible in Josh's room to help comfort him. I'm not sure if he can hear it, but if anything, it has helped minister to us and hopefully others around here in the ICU. Josh's dad Don has been sharing the many ways God has answered our prayers throughout this trial with the staff. It's a good reminder to me too. I'm so thankful for Don being here. He took Noah to stay with him at his hotel, and they got to go to the spa, the heated pool, and have breakfast. Nathan has also enjoyed time with Papa. They miss dad being home.

God is teaching us that we must set our eyes on God's love, sovereignty, and all that He has done in the past. Also, even through the dark days, we see glorious blessings. I'm so thankful for all the help Katelynn is to us at home so I can stay at Josh's bedside. It's easy to be anxious about the many things going wrong with Josh at the hospital, but ultimately we need to do our best to be informed and trust God with the rest. Please pray that Josh and the family would rest in Christ, who gives us the privilege to be children of God. It's easy to be tempted to think God has forgotten us, but He cares about our fears, tears, and suffering.

T-cells seemed to be our only hope for Josh to effectively fight off the aggressive PTLD that came as a result of the transplant. If Josh had been any other patient, they would have administered chemo right away. FA made things more complicated. At one point, I had to give the ICU team literature to teach them the basics of his rare disease. They had no idea the implications of it. I endeavored to make the wisest medical decisions based on my research and data with no medial experience or degree, and with only one doctor who knew more about his disease than me. I felt alone, lost, and confused.

The FA Facebook support group was something I used to try to reach out to others for help. A woman Josh's age in the UK that was fighting the same disease chatted with me online and suggested transporting him to another hospital with more expertise. At that point, I knew any effort to move him would be too late. My comfort at that desperate time was knowing that God was in control and could heal him right where he was if it was His will to do so. Moreover, I realized that even if he was to live for a few more months, his fate was sealed just like this British woman.

The only difference was their eternal destination. Josh's fate for heaven was guaranteed. Hers hung in the balance. I tried sharing with her the hope of Christ and His free gift of eternal life. She seemed too consumed with living the best of the end of her life now, to worry about what would soon follow after. I prayed and shared as much as she'd allow. God only knows how her story ended. She lived a couple more months longer than Josh, and we kept in touch online. Any support from friends at the time was mostly online. We were hundreds of miles away from friends and family. Yet, my God was right by our side through every high and every low turn.

May 1, 2017

Josh got his breathing tube taken out this afternoon. I thank God for this answer to prayer. He has remained in a state of mental confusion. Josh has neither talked nor responded very much. A nurse called his name loudly, and he didn't move a muscle. When the nurse asked him to squeeze his hand, he did not respond either. They are saying that several things could be contributing to this. The first would be ICU delirium, which usually clears up after a few hours, days, or weeks. Other causes could be that his kidneys and liver are adversely affected. There is nothing we can do to help Josh other than pray and wait. We hope he wakes up fully without any further complications. It is a dark road we are traveling through, but God still shows his mercy toward us.

The doctors think there is still hope, so we continue to fight. They may do a liver biopsy through a small incision in his neck because of his low platelets. Unless he is still delirious by tomorrow, then they won't do it since he can't stay still. They want to do more chemo tomorrow because of the aggressive nature of PTLD.

God encouraged me last night after putting the boys to bed. I went out to Trader Joe's to pick up some produce, and the cashier asked me how my day was going. I told her about Josh in the ICU, and the bagger went over and got me some flowers and a bag of dark chocolate peanut butter cups. I bowed my head, closed my eyes and let tears run down my face. The worker handed me the bouquet. I glanced at the cashier's eyes, and they had tears too. They just gave them to me for free. I have a peanut allergy, but Katelynn and the boys enjoyed the chocolate. Katelynn arranged the flowers in a jar in our living room and fixed a ribbon on it. It's a bitter-sweet reminder of God's kindness to all of us. I have been shedding many tears the past couple of days.

The presence of Josh's dad felt like a giant weight lifted off my shoulders. It was hard to communicate over the phone the fullness of what was going on to Josh's mind and body. He was leaving us. It was hard enough to accept it myself and even harder to relay devastating news to his family from afar. Having Josh's dad there for a couple of days was instrumental in making major decisions. He also helped with practical issues that ensued such as getting my car towed out of the hospital parking lot and fixed right away. When he arrived, Josh was unable to speak. His dad spoke tenderly, assured him of his love, and encouraged him in the faith.

We were unsure if Josh could hear. There was a sweet time of mingled joy when we sang a hymn together. His dad and I sang with all our hearts, and our voices could not help but convey our sorrow mixed with joy in the worship of our King. Josh shed a couple of tears at the end. This moment meant the world to us. It showed us that he was still with us in his mind. My beloved heard us singing and was comforted.

May 2, 2016

The swelling from Josh's neck went down almost entirely, which is great news. However, he still is in a state of delirium, either from the sedation at the ICU or from his liver which at this point is continuing to fail. The doctors say that it should go away over time if we can address his liver failing and PTLD. We don't know how long that will take. Josh seemed a little more alert today. When we called his name, he turned his face toward us.

Josh's dad has been an immense help. Today he helped me get my SUV towed from the narrow OHSU parking garage to the auto shop, and back, within one day. The chaplain also came by and talked to us. He is an evangelical Christian and ministered to our aching hearts. Also, I love the social worker. It's so good to have someone who is knowledgeable, genuinely loves people, and is trained to help with the practical things. Even more—who loves God.

My mom will be flying in from LA tomorrow evening. Thank you, mom. Thank you, Dad, Jessica, Ashley, and Alex for doing what it takes to free her up so she can be here for us. Even with the aches of our hearts and the many tears, we have much to give thanks to God for and much to press forward.

Please pray for Josh's liver, for his delirium, and for him not to suffer like this. Due to significant liver problems that have been progressing quickly, they did not start chemo. They gave Josh an anti-inflammatory drug tonight. Tomorrow he will get another dose of Rituximab and steroids. We are hoping Dr. Jewel will be able to get some T-cells very soon. We have not heard a "no", but haven't heard a "yes" regarding the T-cells yet. Even, with a "yes" we need to buy Josh more time since it may take a week for us to get them. Hope is not lost. As long as Josh is breathing, we continue to pray, entrusting ourselves to the Lord's will whatever that may look like. God's Spirit and your prayers sustain us through this trial.

The Necessity of Prayer

I must spend some time in prayer

In the wee hours of the morn

Before the sun announces

That another day is born

I must spend some time in prayer
Forsaking rest and sleep
For it's my meeting with the Lord
An appointment I must keep

I must spend some time in prayer
To set the day a'right
That my motives and actions
Would be pleasing in His sight

I must spend some time in prayer
Interceding for God's own
That both His will and calling
To His people would be known

I must spend some time in prayer
In the presence of His glory
Rehearsing all the deeds
Of His redemption story

I must spend some time in prayer
Confessing my transgression
And be covered by Christ's blood
In Holy intercession

I must spend some time in prayer
Before I begin my day
For there is no greater deed
Than to bow my head and pray

Copyright Joshua "J.D." Seibert 2015

[155]

[Chapter 10]

God Calls my Beloved Home to Eternal Paradise

Josh lay on the hospital bed breathing heavily and sedated. He looked rugged but ever so handsome. His swelling had gone down. Facial hair had grown, and it wasn't gray. He was worried about his hair growing back in white or grey hues after it fell off from the chemo. An old man is what he foresaw himself looking like at the end. To anyone else this man who just had spent a week in the ICU and hadn't eaten, slept, or showered must not have looked like hot stuff. To me, there was a robust, stately and admirable beauty shining through his face. When I looked at him, I saw a beautiful bittersweet image of Christ in His sufferings. His entire body was shutting down. I whispered, "Babe, you're looking good. Your hair is growing back. It will grow back to normal, not gray." There was silence.

The primary BMT doctor knocked on the door and came looking for me. She walked in and closed the door behind her. Josh still lay on the bed hooked up to all the machines, making no noise other than heavy breaths at frequent intervals. I wasn't sure if he was awake or if he could hear our conversation. Nonetheless, his presence gave me confidence. His example drove me to a determination to share the love of Christ with the doctor no matter how hard it would be. Josh was referred to this doctor as a BMT specialist familiar with his disease. I wondered where she had been since complications ensued with some degree of frustration. In the two weeks since he had been admitted back to the hospital, she did not see him or check on him personally. Although she was still involved in the oversight of his care, it was behind the scenes working with Dr. Jewel who had been checking on him on at least a daily basis.

The doctor informed me that, in her medical opinion, she did not believe that Josh would survive much longer. The memory of a similar conversation flashed into my mind. It had been weeks before the transplant. Josh looked at her and asked frankly, "Do you think I have a chance at making it?" She gave him a confident look and affirmed, "I believe you will." The same doctor now said Josh would die. She lamented and was sorry for not anticipating the PTLD or identifying it sooner. The doctor related that the PTLD may have been there all along, or he may have come into the transplant with lymphoma. It seemed like she was trying to make sense of it all in her own mind. After relaying the bad news, she let out tears and repeated the only words left for her to say, "I'm sorry, I'm so sorry." I appreciated her honesty and courage to be upfront about Josh's condition as well as her shortcomings.

God gave me a heart to forgive her. Then, He gave me the opportunity to share the message of true forgiveness and eternal life found in Christ. If nothing else came of it, my own heart was freed from bitterness that pollutes one's spirit and rots the bones in grief. There was not one single person that could have changed things, though we tried earnestly to do our part to fight the disease viciously. His treatment was under divine orders from above. It was God in His sovereign will that chose to call Josh home at such a young age. Nothing any doctor could have possibly done differently could have changed his fate. While her eyes filled with tears, I peacefully responded with the assurance of Josh's heavenly dwelling because of his faith in Jesus. I wondered if Josh could hear our conversation.

If Josh was listening, I thought how he would be proud. Moreover, God was indeed watching, and I believe He was honored.

Josh's body began to quickly shut down until multiple vital organs including his brain, liver, and kidneys failed. He painfully struggled with each breath. The doctors did their best, but ultimately God's will was accomplished working through frail human instruments. We were called to do our best to fight for Josh to have more time on this earth to serve the Lord. We prayed and prayed. Now was the time when we heard the creaking of the door shut, and the words we dreaded to hear: "no." On the evening of May 3rd, the doctor on duty at the ICU told me that Josh would not make it through the night. God had already known the exact number of his days.

Josh had been on many painkillers around the clock to no avail. This was the apex of his suffering. His body got pale, weak, and was now completely deteriorated. His mouth looked like it was being scorched with coals. Josh's kidneys, liver, and brain took the worst hit. Yet, he was still relentlessly fighting. He kept gasping for air. He fought to live even while knowing that to die would be far greater. He was not fighting for himself. He did it for us. The nurse walked into his room again and asked, "Is there anyone he is waiting to say goodbye to?" My mind was puzzled as I thought of who he might want to see. Nathan was too young and the rest of his family was too sick to come. That night Josh did not relent, fighting for every breath.

If only Josh could pull through. It's hard to grasp why God could possibly take him home so soon and in his painful condition. Josh was a wise pastor, a faithful father, and a loving husband. Why him? There was so much potential in Josh. It made no logical sense. He had so much more he wanted to accomplish for the Lord. I rested in God's perfect wisdom, sovereignty, and character. My mind was protected from doubts and rage by my loving Lord and Savior. All that was left for me to do was to thank

Him for His kindness to give me the grace to trust Him with the incomprehensible turn of events.

May 4, 2017 at 3a.m.

> Josh is very ill. His liver continues to do poorly, and now his kidneys are going down real fast. Please pray for a miracle! This is the hardest place to be. We ask for wisdom and peace–ultimately that God's will be done and He gets all glory! Also, please pray Josh wouldn't suffer much more than he's already hurting. Prayers for us to point others to Jesus through this no matter what, and earnest prayers for our boys, Noah and Nathan.

My body, mind, and soul were exhausted on multiple levels from my being by my beloved's bedside all night waiting for him to take his last breath. Josh had been moaning loudly all night as he gasped for air. He relentlessly stayed up trying to catch his breath and keep himself alive. He hadn't slept for days. I hoped he would give in to his fatigue and rest peacefully. As soon as it looked like he calmed down and might fall asleep, he anxiously gasped for more air and moan. All I could do is assure him that all would be well. He moaned and gasped, and I'd say, "Everything's going to be ok my love." This went on for hours. It went on all night.

At last, a doctor came in and wanted to talk to me. Instead of giving me an update of Josh or asking how he had been doing, he asked how I was doing and looked like he was going to order me to leave. The doctor suggested I go home to get some sleep. I decided I better go home, and try to take a power nap. I wanted to return quickly with my mother for moral support in a couple hours to talk to the day-time doctors with a better head on my shoulders.

Shortly after I hit the road, I called a dear sister in Christ that I connected with through a bone marrow transplant support group.

She also worked for a hospital as a social worker. I remember our conversation and how much it meant to me. Her tone was calm and sweet. She knew exactly what was needed. I asked if she could just pray for me, but she asked me to pray instead. She attentively listened as I worked up the energy to put my thoughts into words and give them over to the Lord in prayer. In deep sorrow, I uttered an earnest prayer, "Oh, Heavenly Father. I beg you to please do a miracle and heal Josh. I know you are able, Lord! But I also know that you may be calling him home. If so, please take him quickly so that he no longer has to suffer. Please make it clear what your will for Josh's life is. In Jesus' name." Immediately after uttering the desperate words that were ringing inside my mind, I heard a soft and heartfelt amen on the other end of the phone line.

The minute I walked in the door of our house, I got a call from the hospital asking me how soon I could return because Josh's breathing was getting worse. Complications continued, and Josh experienced full healing in glory instead of in this broken world. As his final time drew to an end, Josh saw heaven as the sun was rising to a new day. May 4th, 2017 at about 5a.m. Josh breathed his last after suffering immensely. God achieved victory for Josh in the eternal sense, through his faith in Christ.

May 4, 2017 at 1 p.m

The doctors had told us Josh may not make it through the night. So I stayed up all night in the small ICU room and tried to comfort him. It was bleak and stressful to see him having a harder and harder time breathing. My heart began to race to the roof and get so anxious, I feared a panic attack would strike. I hadn't slept much for over a week while he was in the ICU. That night I didn't sleep one bit. The clock now read: 5a.m. The doctor took me outside and asked if I was taking care of myself: he was concerned. My mom had just flown into town and was at home with the boys sleeping, yet I haven't seen her. So I ended up deciding to make a it back home briefly to pick up my mom and try to nap for an hour or so, then return with my mom before the doctors got there.

Before I left the hospital I prayed with Josh knowing it may be the last time. On my way home I called a friend who's gone through a BMT transplant with her husband and we prayed for God's will to be made clear because I didn't know what to do. I was in agony watching Josh suffer and his whole body begin to shut down. When I got home, the hospital called and asked me how long it would take me to get back. Then, a minute later, they said Josh had passed. I knew he went home to be with the Lord for full healing. It was about 5:20am just as the sun was rising.

My mom and I drove back to the hospital where Josh's body looked so different, but in a good way! He had a little smile on his face and bright glow that just seemed so peaceful, as if he had seen Christ. The nurse said that right after I prayed with him and left, his heart rate and blood pressure got worse until his heart stopped beating. He may have been holding on for me. Part of me was glad to see him free from his frail body and knowing he is now with the Lord! Yet, my heart still aches and can't stop beating fast. I have not been able to rest or eat at all. I feel sick to my stomach. Please pray for the peace that surpasses all understanding in Christ for our family. Pray for the boys to not doubt God's love and be filled with comfort. May we all be comforted with the promise in Scripture of eternal life that is free to all who believe in the Son of God. "For God so loved the world that he gave his only begotten son that whoever believes in him will not perish but have everlasting life." John 3:16

I will post more updates regarding memorial services. Josh wanted two–one in our church in Merlin and one in CA with family and friends there. Thank you!"

Josh passed from suffering to glory. The morning the Lord took Josh home was one I'll never forget. I hung up, and my mom found me just sitting on the bed... stunned. She knew. The next thing I heard was her loud wailing, "No, it can't be, you're too young!" She held me and cried. Although tears now flood my eyes as I write and recount these harsh memories, the tears could not flow from my weary eyes that moment while my mom held me with a tight grip. Part of me could not believe what had happened.

We drove back to the hospital to find Josh's body cold and lifeless, yet at peace. There was an unexplainable glow to his face and even a little smile. Surprisingly, my heart was filled with incomprehensible joy. The first thing I did was wonder what it must have been like for him to see Jesus and heaven open up to receive him into glory. The young doctor came in to explain how it happened. I only heard half of what he said but responded with the good news of the gospel and a calm, peaceful spirit. I looked up at the doctors and said, "It is ok, he is now with Jesus." God knew it would happen. It was pre-ordained in His book all the days Josh would live before one came to be.

When my mom saw his stiff dead body, she started reciting the Hail Mary out loud to plead her for his soul. It broke my heart. I begged, "Please stop." Inside, I wanted to yell at the top of my lungs, "He's not here; he has risen!" All my mom has ever known is to pray to Mary after the death of a loved one. I explained to her that Josh's soul was already in heaven because of his faith in the perfect mediator—Jesus Christ. He was immediately ushered into the glory of heaven. It was hard for her to understand how I could be so sure. The reason for my confidence is from God's Word. He promises to grant eternal life to all who would believe in the name of His Son, and in Him alone for salvation. This same gospel message was the main love of Josh's life. He loved to tell the story of unseen things above—of Jesus and His glory, of Jesus and His love. He did so till the very end. Even while in the hospital, going through the worst suffering of his life, Josh's faith in Christ didn't waver and kept him strong. "The arm of the flesh can never save us from troubles. When the godly entrust themselves to God, however, he will empower then to stand strong in their troubles and deliver them to safety." (Lawson, p. 32). The same faith in Christ kept me grounded too.

After spending some time in that hospital room where Josh's dead body lay still and became stiffer by the minute, a new social worker came to ask if we had made arrangements with a funeral home. I was speechless. The thought had never crossed my mind. Not knowing where to go or what to do, I prayed. Then, I called Pastor Ken from Clackamas Bible Church where we were staying. He expressed sincere condolences and kindly referred me to a local family-owned funeral home that most of their church members use. They knew precisely what to do, were very professional, and sympathetic. Josh wished to spare the family of an extra financial burden by asking to be cremated. I was thankful not to have to make another dreadful decision on the spot, nor many others that would come with an hourglass, like trying to figure out how to transport his body. When I had asked Josh if he wanted to be buried, he said he would leave that decision up to me. I was glad for the extra time to pray and make that decision. It took much prayer and talking to others widows, but eventually, I was led to bury his ashes at a local cemetery for the children's sake.

Part of me couldn't believe I was holding my husband's ashes. Perhaps I had been naively hopeful. Yet, I don't know how anyone could possibly accept the departure of such a loved one. Josh was a faithful instrument of God. With every last word, he demonstrated a passion for sharing the gospel truth and dependence on Christ. God answered many prayers along the way and used suffering for His glory and our good. Josh was now absent from the body and present with the Lord.

News got out. I wanted the immediate family to find out personally so I made some phone calls and waited until the afternoon to post the news on social media. Later, most of our distant friends and family heard of Josh's home-going via the blog. It was a relief for me to be able to share in one place and not to have to repeat it over and over and be asked a thousand painful questions. It was a touchy time. I appreciated the love and encouragement from others, while at the same time I needed some time to myself to process everything too. The day the Lord took him home, I went for a walk around our neighborhood alone. It felt like spring had just begun since being cooped up in a hospital. All around me flowers bloomed. Fully, I thought about Josh blooming now in heaven. It gave me much comfort to know that he was now free from suffering, and in the greatest of places. Some comforted me with Scriptures about heaven. The best thing others could do was to give us their faithful and much-needed prayers. The prayers were felt and evidenced by the grace that was abundantly lavished on us.

May 7, 2017

The past four days have been full of tears, headaches, and nausea from missing my beloved and closest friend and the man I had the privilege to call my husband. It breaks my heart. Part of me cannot believe what has actually happened. On the other hand, my senses and painful memories of the hospital sober me to the reality of his passing. My hope comes from him going into the arms of Jesus. Josh is in heaven because of his unwavering faith in Christ, not because he was a "good" person or performed enough good deeds to save himself, "for all have sinned and fall short of the glory of God, and are justified by his grace as a gift, through the redemption that is in Christ Jesus, whom God put forward as a propitiation by his blood, to be received by faith." Romans 3:23-25.

Thoughts of Josh enjoying the splendor of God and being free from sin and from his physically ill body bring sweet repose. Yet, it still hurts to lose him here on this earth. The boys sorely miss their daddy. At night before bed or before naps, Nathan says in a faint voice out loud, "I want my Daddy!" He sits on my lap, and I tell him it's OK to cry. I also tell him about what beautiful place heaven is. Nathan asks me if we can cry together. Yesterday, the little guy said he wanted to go to heaven so he can see Daddy and asked if he would be able to hug him and play cars with him there. In these difficult moments, I have the privilege of sharing with my children the Way God has made for us to get to heaven through Jesus who died on the cross to pay the penalty for our sins. Noah wanted to see Daddy, so he looked through pictures of him. Please pray for the boys to be convinced of the love of God despite His seeming absence. God is ever-present and cares so much for our tears and fears. So many people have come alongside us and helped carry the burden of our loss. Please continue to pray for the Noah and Nathan. Ultimately pray for their salvation, that they would have the hope of being reunited again in heaven one day through the perfect life of Jesus.

Our Eternal Weight of Glory

When we reflect in circumspect
Upon a man, we loved so dear
It helps us see the legacy
That he made while he was here

And though he's gone, it lives on
Enshrined upon our heavy hearts
His impact will remain intact
Long after his soul departs

And this we know, that all saints go
Where the Christian graduates
Far from the strife of earthly life
Where their heavenly home awaits

Where resurrection and perfection
Will transform their humble tent
And they'll be His and like He is
No longer with a sinful bent

Betrothed and immortally clothed
They'll meet their Husband in the air
And hearing His voice, they'll rejoice
At the sound of the trumpets blare

So though we part, we don't lose heart
Nor do we grieve as others grieve
For we'll be raised by the Ancient of Days
With an inheritance to receive

Copyright Josh "J.D." Seibert 2011

[Chapter 11]

Joy in the Aftermath of Tragedy

I n one sense, Josh experienced full healing. He no longer
suffers from physical ailments, the corruption of the flesh
and sin. We take joy knowing that Josh is in heaven, not
because of the good deeds he did. When weighed against the
commandments God holds us accountable to, no one could ever
earn entrance to heaven. Josh is in heaven because Jesus paid the
penalty for every sin Josh could never repay. It is because of our sin
that we all deserve death forever, yet it is the gift of God through
Jesus that we can obtain eternal life. Jesus was Josh's substitute on
the cross, taking the punishment we all deserve. The God of the
universe became a man, died for our sin on the cross, was buried,
and rose from the grave. In his resurrection, we have eternal life!
Josh's faith became sight. He now possesses eternal life.

May 9, 2017

It has been almost a week since Josh went home to the
Lord. The last couple of days have had their ups and
downs. There have been lots of tears shed, many cries of
prayers heard, and cherished memories replayed over and
over again. We are trying to take it day by day and make
time to process, pray, and grieve through many things. We
grieve for the loss of a loving father, godly husband, faithful friend, gentle shepherd, solid pastor, wise teacher, full
provider, and sweet daily companion. I think and often

talk about Josh in the heavenly places. I also try to en-joy the relationships we still have here on earth, especially with the boys. I have been blessed to have both my mom and Katelynn with me this week. Thank you, mom, and thank you, Katelynn. I don't think I could do this without you! Also, thank you all who are praying earnestly for us. I definitely can't do this without God's grace to sustain me and to give me strong faith, courageous hope, and agape love to pass on to the boys.

Today was a day marked with peace. Praise the Lord! We all went out to the Portland Zoo for the day. It was not the same without Josh, but I can say that we enjoyed each other and the beautiful animals God created. Some of my favorite moments were watching Nathan crawl around the floor and pretend he was an elephant or to watch Noah excited to be able to hold his breath through the long tun-nel at the end of the train ride. We talked about how one day in the new heaven animals like the bear or the lion will be able to play with us and even cuddle. Heaven is a sweet comfort for us.

Despite the amazing grace of God to sustain our faith, grief was a painful process for our entire family. It started to take its course at the onset of Josh's diagnosis. The climax of our sorrow came the week Josh died. We did not mourn as the world that has no hope. Throughout our grief journey, we saw God's hand and learned to smile and laugh again. One thing Josh taught us is that laughing makes it easier to navigate the storms of life. God miraculously worked to begin to heal us of the shock of saying goodbye to one so dear and beloved. "Because He 'looked away' from His suffer-ing to the 'joy that was set before Him,' you can rest peacefully in the truth that joy is assured to you, too. As you set your gaze on the one who fixed His eyes resolutely on the joy of pleasing His

Father, you'll find that same pleasure filling your heart." (Fitzpatrick, 45).

God blessed our family with joy in our sorrow, and answered prayers for peace. He used the truth from Scripture, prayer, and the church to accomplish this. Studying God's Word, and mediating on His sovereign character was the life-saver that rescued me from drowning in a sea of gloom. It was a sweet balm to my soul to remain surrounded by the love of the church. Writing in the blog helped me process and share what was going on inside. It was not only an emotional outlet; it was a medium I used to turn a tragedy into an opportunity for the gospel. This door into the hearts of others was golden. It gave meaning to the incomprehensible pain. In some ways, it reflected the beauty of the cross whereby a tragic death, could impact the good of others.

May 12, 2017

We are with prayers, love, compassion, and support from the church body. The Lord has answered many prayers for peace and strength for our family. Many have kindly sent flowers, messages, and cards. We've even had several send meals. One of Josh's best friend's growing up brought some snacks and cards for us. Other friends came over yesterday evening and brought us dinner. We've enjoyed fellowship with loved ones and sharing memories of Josh. Pastor Ken took Noah on a hike today to a site Noah's been eager to see—Multnomah Falls.

Although losing my husband has been the most challenging thing I've ever been called to bear, God's grace and mercy are carrying us through. Yesterday I picked up Josh's ashes and death certificates, and it was a sobering reminder of our great loss. Nevertheless, I sensed not only God's presence, but in some way, Josh's as well. It was a gloomy day. Nathan and Noah woke up in the middle of the night. Nathan was so sad and scared that I might not be there. I came into his room and assured him I was there. I just held him and prayed with him. He went back to sleep joyful remembering being outside our Grants Pass home with the BBQ grilling hamburgers with daddy. He kept saying, "I loved that!"

We miss Josh immensely! I have dreams of seeing him again. Please continue to pray for us as we mourn the loss of such a godly father who was so committed to the lives of his children, family, and church flock. Josh did not go without a fight. Till the last day, he fought with all his might for his life, because of his great love for God, our family, and our church. The BMT was his only chance at saving his life. He knew the risk of complications involved. The last way he would have chosen to go is at a hospital. Yet, he endured suffering and lay down his will before God. It reminds me of so much of Christ and his great love for us that drove him to the cross. "Greater love hath no man than this that a man lay down his life for his friends." John 15:13.

I rest in God's sovereignty over the length of Josh's life. Psalm 139 is a continual comfort to me when tempted with doubts. God knew every single day Josh would live before he was even born. Most people with FA only live to age 33, so we were blessed with the four sweet years we did get to be with Josh. Our comfort comes from knowing that God is good and loves us and knows the answers to our "whys?" God is all-knowing, always good, and proves faithful. He is with us till the end of the age, through Jesus and His Spirit that indwells believers. Furthermore, it is the Holy Spirit that moves the church to respond with such love as it has with us. It is a living testament to the authenticity of the Christian faith.

The weeks that followed were tremendously challenging but at the same time ones filled with God's grace to meet us at every station. First, we had to move from Portland back to Merlin and then try to figure out where we would go from there. My mom stayed with us for a few days and then flew back to Los Angeles. Katlynn, our nanny needed to return home. Shortly after that, I was left with the boys… alone. We had said goodbye to our new church friends from Portland. I then had to decide if we would say farewell to our church family in Merlin too. Josh and I had planned to spend the rest of our lives in Oregon. We loved our church in Merlin and wanted to serve there until Josh retired. We dreamed of growing old together there—sitting outside our patio in our rocking chairs watching our grandchildren play outdoors. What would our lives look like now that he was gone? There were so many decisions to be made. I had grown used to making decisions with Josh. He was my head. I had a say so on matters, but he made the final call. I felt like a chicken with its head cut off. Who would advise me when I didn't know what to do? I had to turn to Christ as my head, and His body, the church, as the arms that upheld us.

May 17, 2017

The last few days have been a whirlwind. We arrived safely home on Sunday evening. The Lord gave us clear skies, and we made great timing! We had church family waiting for us at home to help us unload and make the transition smoother. After unloading all our stuff, which we barely fit back into our SUV, we rushed out to the Bolan's house for a lovely dinner. We arrived just in time to Live Stream The Master's Seminary's graduation ceremony at Grace Community Church to catch the short tribute that

John MacArthur did for Josh. Thanks, Pastor John, Ray Mehringer, and Grace Community Church!

It made a difference to have our friends and church family surround us as we walked through the doors of our home. The hardest part for me was walking into our bedroom where at the head of our bed we had framed a family life 'Marriage Covenant' certificate in the middle of two frames; one with an engagement picture of Josh and I dressed in cowboy attire, and the other being the most recent family photo taken out by the pond Josh loved to fish. The Lord has been answering your prayers for peace. While, I still have my moments where I yearn for Josh; more often, I've been able to cherish the memories and not dwell on the sorrow of his loss. I have so much to be thankful for, and so much I learned for our four years of marriage. Honestly, I mourn more when I see the boys hurting for their daddy. I also feel like I have seen other people ache for me. I can't even really understand it. Thus, it has to be from the Lord. Thank you to everyone who is helping me carry this burden. I don't bear it alone. It's first Christ that carries me, but then he uses His people in tangible ways.

The next day was Nathan's 3rd birthday. We still had much to unpack, and Nathan had a nasty cold. The poor little guy was miserable most of the day. He was full of sorrow and just wanted to lay in bed and cried for daddy. Noah at the end of the day helped me bake him gluten and dairy free cake, put several home-made pizzas in the oven. We had two sets of church family grandparents join us for dinner and cake. It cheered him up! We made it into a little birthday family gathering. Our friend has organized a birthday party with his little friends this Friday at a local park, and a meal train for our family. The Lord has His arms around us through his body, the church!

Our church is busy preparing for Josh's memorial service. Our church submitted an obituary column for Josh in the Daily Courtier. I was asked to do the eulogy. I am thankful for that opportunity but appreciate your prayers on this. I witnessed the ten year old daughter of a fellow home school mom give a eulogy for her mom. If she could do it, so should I.

Josh's memorial service was just perfect. It honored Josh and his Savior best. If Josh could see it, he would be pleased. His passion was for others to hear the saving message of Christ. The gospel was clearly presented at the memorial. It was such an encouragement to see how many people from our church and the community filled the large sanctuary room. Many shared from their heart of all the work God accomplished through Josh in their life. Our neighbor came to our church for the first time and shared how he saw God bring Josh to earthly paradise in our Oregon quintessential home. As an outsider, he was able to observe how Josh went from earthly paradise to heavenly paradise. It could not be further from the truth. It did my soul much good to listen to all the testimonies of Josh's impact and to personally get on the mic and share his eulogy. More importantly, the gospel was front and center. It was the message that Pastor Mike shared. In every testimony, Josh's life so loudly proclaimed Christ.

After the service, people were asking questions, "What next? Where will you live?" Josh and I had only briefly talked about what I'd do if he passed. Josh instructed me to move back to Los Angeles with family and go back to Grace Community Church, where we met while he was in seminary. Moving in with family was not an easy option as we had rashly assumed. It was daunting to think about returning to LA on my own, where the housing market had skyrocketed enormously high. In many ways, we were ill prepared to part ways. It was a shock to think of living life on our own again with two boys now and without Josh who had been our earthly provider. I had to remember that God remained Jehovah Jireh who would provide for all our needs. Indeed, He was always one step ahead of us without me realizing it. In the beginning, I could not see anything past the mired fog in front of me. I had to take leaps of faith forward into an unknown life that had engulfed our little family.

May 22, 2017

The memorial service at Merlin Church was beautiful. I somehow made it through the eulogy without crying. I'm so thankful for the leadership and help with everything from our sweet church. The pews filled up, and the gospel proclaimed. It was an encouragement to see our neighbor who doesn't usually come to church come and share about how he'll miss Josh's crazy fishing out by our ponds in the rain and snow.

Sunday service for the first time at our church without Josh was difficult. I wanted to see him as usual. It was sad to have him missing. Noah looked withdrawn, and I felt lost. I got used to bringing Josh a power smoothie and sitting up in the front to support him. Now church is not the same. It is still a sweet place because it's filled with God's Spirit-filled people who have become family. Our church and community has embraced us and poured out their love on us. We've been getting meals delivered to our house every day. Two older men from our church took Noah out fishing on a boat at the lake the other day. So many have reached out to us in different ways.

Today, our dear friends took us on a guided boat ride down the Rouge River. It was breath-taking. God's creation is just stunning. We saw a bald eagle and several different birds. It was the hottest day thus far at 93 degrees.

The boys and I miss their daddy! Nathan has nights like tonight where he especially misses Daddy before bed. He finds comfort in me holding him, sometimes crying together, and talking about things in his three-year-olds vocabulary kind if way. Noah misses having a father figure.

The other day a church friend relayed that the biblical meaning of being comforted means to be with strength. The Lord comforts me with the promises of his abounding love toward the fatherless and the widow. While I can't tangibly see with my physical eyes, by faith, I envision God doing good and unexpected things as he works to comfort and provides for us. Please pray for wisdom as I seek the Lord's will. The call to make decisions for our family now is overwhelming.

My mind was blown away with a deep sense of awe at how much peace God supplies for our time of need. I anticipated a panic attack, or that my health would fail. Amazingly, neither of those things happened. Caring for the boys and being a rock to them kept me clinging to my Rock when times were incredibly difficult. Furthermore, the comfort I received from God compelled me to comfort others. I sought to be an example to the church and those watching.

At the same time, I did not want to do damage by ignoring the scars that were cut deep into my heart. When I was alone with God, I let Him have all my tears. His Word comforted me by telling me He stores each teardrop in a bottle (Ps 56:8.) I wept, grieved, and mourned. However, I did not stay there. I had to be completely honest with God about my hurts, and then let Him wipe my tears with His truth. I surrendered my broken dreams and picked up my cross to follow Christ's example, and similarly lead others.

May 27, 2017

The last couple of days have been a reality check. It's not that I have been denying Josh's passing into heaven. However, I've been keeping my grief in check by not dwelling on the sorrow too much. While this can be so helpful in keeping everything going for our little family, it may also keep me from grieving healthily. Thus, I have been opening up to the Lord about my disappointments and taking time in prayer to talk to him about my grief and allowing myself to have sorrow and lay it before him. Recently, I received in the mail a pleasant surprise—a package from Clackamas Bible Church with part one of four booklets on grieving and included a note reminding me that our little family will remain in their prayers. They plan on mailing the rest throughout the next couple of months. That means a lot to me. The Lord is using his global Church body to care for us in many ways.

I wish things for our family could go back to how they were. The lovely country home we are currently renting is still peaceful, yet feels lonely. We miss Josh on so many levels. Simple things he used to do can sometimes be hard, like starting the lawn mower. Although, God's Word assures us even this is all for our good. During fatal blows, it's hard to understand this truth humanly. It's only by faith that we can hold on to God's promises and cling to his unfailing love. His love was demonstrated in how he freely gave up his only son to die on the cross for people like us, who never deserved it at all. We have all sinned and fall short of God's standard none of us deserves to enter heaven. God's limitless love made way for us to enter his courts above.

Despite my faith, it still hurts. The pain is real, and as I ponder all our hopes and dreams for our family, it breaks my heart that we will not be able to fulfill them together. I also realize that through this storm God will work powerfully in pulling me closer to Christ and depending on Him and his people. He wants to renew my strength and change my desires to want him above all earthly things. He will grant joy and hope for the unknown future. God promises to comfort the broken-hearted.

Our church family has been so supportive in many ways. We've been keeping busy enjoying fellowship with the saints. Yesterday, we got to spend a fun day at Lake of the Woods on Tahiti boats. Even Nathan wanted to stay in the water and fearlessly climb the boats. Today we went out to the Indian Mary Park with a few other families for a BBQ and games. It helps the kids cope to get out of the house. The boys are still struggling, each in his own ways. Nathan gets sad and misses daddy frequently. Noah tries to be tough. Many have surrounded us and continue to pour out much love on the boys.

The Church never quite had such a sweet fragrance to me till this season of my life. As a pastor's wife engulfed in a life of ministry, sometimes the church didn't always look so pretty. I now have a deeper appreciation for religion in its purest described in James 1:26 as visiting orphans and widows in their affliction.

We are all still a work in progress till we reach glory. Josh is now enjoying this awesome glory unhindered by his earthly body. We've been very interested in reading books about heaven. We got some kids books on heaven like Randy Alcorn's Heaven for Kids which helped the boys get a better picture of where Daddy is now.

Our church was an immense fortress of protection against all that threatened to undo our broken family further. They shared the burden of our heavy grief and made it lighter. It was surprising to find that those whom we didn't think were close to us before, reached out and helped the most. We had meals delivered to us. Some offered to watch the boys. Others offered to do yard work. Hundreds of the people provided many prayers to God on our behalf. A handful of dear saints did the hard job of being emotionally involved.

Fear gripped me from the first night I had to sleep alone in our bedroom at our secluded home in Paradise Ranch. My mind kept replaying what I could do if a burglar came in. It was overwhelming to think about not only having to protect myself but the kids. We had rats in our country abode, and they made noises late at night that sounded like a break-in. The sound awakened and frightened me to the point where I could not go back to sleep. I hardly slept some nights. A sweet friend who knew my struggle called every night to make sure I was ok. She gave me the freedom to call her at any time of the night. One night a dear woman from our church slept on the couch so I could get some sleep. Overall, the church stayed by our side and kept us busy by taking the boys out or inviting us places.

June 2, 2017

Today I got to take a little bit of a coffee break, or caffeinated tea since I'm not a coffee drinker, by myself thanks to our friend Catherine who graciously watched the boys. I got to spend some time getting encouragement from another widow who loves the Lord plus I got to spend some time alone and write a little bit. For me writing is therapeutic and a way to journal this journey and hopefully even in some way encourage others. It's comforting to know that people love us, follow the blog, and continue to pray for our family's specific needs.

Memorial Day was fun. A sweet homeschool family invited us to the river to watch the boat races. Noah picked up his favorite racer number 200 and happily won. The kids enjoyed playing in the river with the other kids.

The last few days I've been busy organizing and trying to get rid of as many things we don't need as possible for the church's upcoming annual garage sale. I've been forced to go through Josh's stuff, which has been a blessing in disguise. Some days have been harder than others. Thursday was four weeks since the Lord took Josh home—that day I cried and struggled with memories of him at the hospital. Last night Nathan woke up missing Daddy and saying he was hungry, so we looked at his pictures while he ate. We often think of how much fun daddy is having in heaven and talk about it. I hope that the boys grow up with a high view of God and heaven as a result of all of this.

Merlin Church has been so supportive of our little family. I see God's loving hand in bringing us out here to such a loving family. Praise God for his provisions and how the church is taking care of us physical as well. They had invested in a retirement plan for the pastors here, and to our surprise, this company is helping us, even after only a short time. The Lord has been very kind to us. Thank you Merlin Church, and all who have donated.

Nights are more challenging as it gets lonely and tempts me toward anxiety. I've been reading Psalms and spending time with my forever husband—Jesus, and that has helped! I greatly enjoy reading. I'm currently reading Elisabeth Elliot's book, *Path of Loneliness*.

Some highlights from my reading:

"For who is like God, but the Lord? And who is a rock, except our God?–the God who equipped me with strength and made my way blameless. He made my feet like the feet of a deer and set me secure on the heights." Psalms 18:31-33

"It often happens that those whose loss is greatest receive the greatest share of grace, mercy, and peace. This does not mean that they never cry, of course. But they do not collapse. Those who only watch and pray and try to put themselves in the place of the bereaved find it almost unendurable. Sometimes they weep uncontrollably, for their imaginations never include the grace." (*The Path of Loneliness*, Elisabeth Elliot)

Our major prayer needs are the following:

1. For the boys—to receive the gift of faith, and be convinced of God's love for them. Also, for godly and encouraging friendships.

2. For continued financial provisions—for God to make his will clear as to our future.

3. For our family—to get into a good routine and learn to function in our new normal without Josh in a way that would make the best use of our time and honor God!

4. For Merlin Church—their search for a new pastor. For them to bring a strong man of God to shepherd the flock Josh loved and left behind.

God answered all these prayers. The boys survived the first year without Josh relatively well. Each of them dealt with the grief differently. Little Nathan expressed his sadness and would often cry and wanted to be held. Growing Noah became more and more frustrated. He began to go through puberty and needed his dad more than ever. Noah would not want to be seen crying, but expressed his anger. It was a rare opportunity when he opened up to anyone about his feelings. Noah told me he could not wrap his mind around why a good God would allow this all to happen. We had several men come alongside of the boys, Noah in particular. The family pastor of the church in Portland took Noah out one-on-one for some ice cream and talked to him about this question. Noah received an "I don't know why" answer, to his question of why God had to take Josh, from a pastor who assured him of what we can bank on—God's goodness and love despite whatever happens in this life. He then witnessed the kindness of God in His provisions.

It was tempting to stay in Merlin; but the snowy winters and distance from family drove me to seek shelter on the southern California coast. My conviction was to stay at home with the boys and to be close to family. It was what Josh would have wanted. He worried and prayed for us to be financially secure if he were to leave us. Finances were an obstacle to finding a place to settle back home in LA. The church, on their initiative, took a generous love offering and continued to pay Josh's salary for three months to give me ample time to plan our unexpected future. Behind the scenes, the church staff worked with their retirement organization to ensure the boys and I were well provided. The love and support we received on behalf of Josh were overwhelming.

Although he was only the pastor for less than a year, the unanimous sentiment of the elders and congregation was the profound and eternal impact on so many in such a short period. Everyone in the church was touched. Their love and appreciation not only for Josh but for the Lord despite our loss, was displayed in how they tangibly loved us. The irony is that before his transplant Josh taught our church through 1, 2, and 3 John on how our love for one another assures us of our faith. Then, our church put their love on display and lived out their faith in Christ through loving us. The boys and I reaped the fruit of God's Word and His and Josh's work in their lives.

The Lord answered our prayers for financial provision through the generosity, love, and support of the church at large as well as our home church where Josh pastored. People all around the world gave what they could, some a couple of dollars while others gave hundreds. Love flooded our weary hearts. Thousands of dollars came in support from the online fundraiser. Also, our church in Merlin gave us a hefty love offering upon our departure and covered all our moving expenses. A church retirement plan supplied a large unexpected check. Other surprisingly amazing things happened. I thought I would soon have to figure out how to return to work. Then, the next thing I knew more money came in. I was left speechless and in awe at how God provided abundantly beyond what I asked or imagined (Eph 3:20). At the end of the year, we were amazingly able to buy a home near family in LA, which allowed me to stay at home with the kids.

By God's grace, we established a bitter-sweet new normal. The normalcy fluctuated with various moves and the chaos of life. We slowly learned to function without our strong leader—our rock. Christ became an even more vivid Rock to us as I had to cling to Him. God placed different people in our lives for seasons when we needed them. A generous couple hosted us in their home and helped with our transition into our own house in LA.

Merlin Church sought a new pastor for only a few months. They called a musically talented new pastor from Texas with his family of six to shepherd the flock. The associate pastor did a superb job transitioning everyone after Josh's medical treatment. However, he waited to retire. The church needed someone to step into a permanent senior pastor role. The previous pastor had served faithfully for nearly 30 years. He came back to preach after Josh's home-going. His message helped many of us process what had happened and pointed us back to the good purposes of God that we might never know.

Blessed Heirs

Though sin still taints

Us Christian saints

Christ's righteousness affords the price

Though weak and frail

And prone to fail

God's grace continues to suffice

For Sons of God

Birthed of sod

His blessed righteousness He shares

From election

To perfection

He regards us His chosen heirs

Whilst the Spirit groans

And creation moans

We await our appointed King

Our blessed adoption

Is not our option

And for this, our hearts do sing!

Copyright Josh "J.D." Seibert 2010

[Chapter 12]

Lingering Questions Silenced by God's Faithfulness

———◆•◆———

There is no logical explanation as to why Josh had to die so young and leave our family suffering in this way. It is tempting even for Christians to doubt God at times when life doesn't make any sense, humanly speaking. It takes resolute faith to believe God is still who He says He is. Remembering God's benevolence, wisdom, and authority, matched by my blessed position in Christ, kept my mind from sinking into doubts. Moreover, it sprang a Spirit-empowered thankful heart that saw each answer to prayer as a monumental reminder of God's eternal love. The unbeliever and the Christian hardened by unbelief, alike blame God for suffering. A dear family member told me to stop praying to my God when he heard the news of Josh's death. My reply is: trust God. "Trust God in the dark. We are safer with him in the dark than without him in the sunshine. He will not suffer your foot to stumble. His rod and his staff never break. Why he brought us here we know not now, but we shall know hereafter. At the end of the gloomy passage beams heavenly light. Then comes the exceeding and eternal weight of glory!" (Cuyler, *32*).

I praise God for all the myriads of "small" answers to prayer that we saw throughout our journey. The last day we attended Merlin Church, my dad kindly traveled 700 miles to the Merlin Church to express his thankfulness. He got in front of the church, moved to tears in gratitude for all that the church had done to make sure our family would be taken care of even after we left Oregon. The love of the church and the answers to our prayer for financial provisions they provided showcased just one reason why I continue to pray to my God—He is faithful.

June 15, 2017

These past days have been so busy that I've scarcely had time to gather my thoughts on the blog. There is a daily "to do" list that doesn't seem ever to get fully completed. The most important thing is that 'God's will be done on earth, as it is in heaven'. Yesterday morning as I started to tackle my list and organize some of Josh's stuff, I just ended up laying on the floor in tears. It wasn't my plan, but God's plan for my day–to spend time crying out to Him.

Thankfully we finished homeschooling for the year. Noah did great–he got straight A's and scored well on his Stanford test. The only reason he was able to finish strong was his self-discipline and Katelynn teaching him. Katelynn was such a wonderful blessing and would be faithful to help Noah with schoolwork–even Math.

I also thank God that loving church family and friends surround us—whether in person, in cyberspace, or over the phone. One of the things I miss the most is having Josh here to talk to every day. We would share almost everything. Now, that he's gone, there's a void in my heart. It's like being sick. I feel weak, and my heart aches—it's empty. During times like this, the Lord calls me to come to Him to fill my cup, and even overflow to others around us.

It's not always easy. Sometimes, I feel like I have a dark cloud come over me and all I see is what's directly in front, staring me in the face—death. It may tempt me to despair and be self-focused. A friend graciously reminded me that the trials we face are not about us. It just hit me. All of this is about God and His purposes.

It's hard to understand God's ways and accept them as gifts to grow us when they come as trials knocking on our door, instead of our neighbor's. Scripture keeps us grounded. The Bible tells us to count them all joy (James 1:2). His ways are not our own (Is 55:8). We are not our own; we were bought with a price–the blood of Jesus (1Cor 6:18-19). I've resigned myself to trusting Him and resting in the not knowing. In our weakness, he is shown strong (2Cor 12:9).

Even though we may not be privy to what God is going to accomplish through our trials, we can run to the arms of our Father who does. He loves us as his children with a fierce love that did not let the cross stop him from pursuing an intimate relationship with us forever. His love is not based on anything we have to offer. It's a love that doesn't even make much sense, as angels can't even fathom it. His love is purely a part of who God is in his essence and being. Even in our frailty and sinfulness, we can't lose God's love. We may forfeit the blessing of being used by Him, but we will never lose His love nor be outside of His grasp.

The days pass quickly, yet the nights can go by slowly as I lay awake sometimes for hours trying to sleep. There are times, just as I'm about to fall asleep, I hear loud noises coming from the kitchen or unknown part of the house. We are renting an old house in the country, and we have some furry little mice and rat friends that make a racket at night. Josh used to hunt them down with his pellet gun.

It can be frightening to be a woman alone at night. I've noticed that my hard days usually translate into difficult nights. I wonder how much of my anxiety is related to grief. I read quote by C.S. Lewis that says, "No one ever told me that grief felt so like fear." With God's help, I'll continue to strive to overcome my fear. The truth is God is my protector and sends his angels to watch over us at night. In His grace to me, we have neighbors and friends close by ready to help at any time, and I just learned we have security patrolling the area every night.

The kids experienced the downpour of grief too. The other day we were driving in the car, and a song about heaven came on. As the words rang in our ears, Nathan exclaimed, "That's where Daddy is!" Praise God Nathan is excited about knowing Daddy is in heaven. Last night he woke up at midnight crying out, "Daddy, daddy?" It saddens me not to be able to do anything other than holding him tight. Nathan understands Daddy is in heaven and grieves in his toddler way. Noah is also grieving in his own "big boy" way too. I'm thankful for moments where he has opened up to me, and we've mourned together.

Though we as Christians still grieve, we have hope that we will see Josh in heaven. Josh also lives on in our hearts forever. He left a storehouse of sermons, poems, stories, and jokes etched in our hearts. The riches he taught, reverberate back from time to time at the moment most needed. I find myself saying the things he used to say or doing the things he did. As a result of being his primary disciple, I resemble him and Christ more. The same goes for the boys too. We are not the same from having Josh. He taught our children God's ways and walked them upward by Christ-like example. He eternally changed all those of us that had the privileged to know him. Now, Josh sees Jesus and is like He is (1John 3:2).

We as Christians long for the day when we will see Jesus and be purified like He is. Furthermore, our earthly goodbye is only temporal. Christ gives his followers eternal exuberant life. Thus we have ample reasons to praise God even in grief.

July 8, 2017

God's goodness has been thoroughly impressed upon my heart this past week. It's like being kissed by Jesus as He leans close to show his love and works on wiping away my tears and giving me new hope. God's love is displayed through the love of others, the answers to prayers, and the simple pleasures of life we can sometimes take for granted. For example, during a recent trip to the beach, I was able to relish feeling the warmth of the sun shining on my shoulders while the soft sand slipped between my toes and the fresh sea water washed the sand away. It's all about perspective. This life will never be perfect; if it were, we probably wouldn't desire heaven or even God himself. Maybe we would get too comfortable here on earth despite it not being our eternal home. However, the beauties, joys, and pleasures of this life are meant to be a sweet glimpse of the glory to come. It should all excite us and lift us.

If we choose joy, determine in our hearts not to let the inevitable inconveniences or disappointments in our lives rob us of our blessing, then we receive the reward of seeing the goodness of the Lord every day. Even on the hard days. Every day is a gift from God. The ultimate gift is Christ himself! One way or another—whether through trials or happiness, the Father wants to give us more of Jesus. We need to have the eyes to see Him and how he works in all things for our good and his glory. I have appreciated having friends point me to Jesus during times when things look bleak. I also want to be that friend to draw others to Christ. Until we get to glory, we can never get too good at loving people better, just as we can never love the Lord enough.

Nonetheless, we can pursue it! Something I've grown to savor is the thought of heaven as a place where all our relationships will be perfect — first, our relationship with Christ. Then, our relationship with each other.

Even though life is so hard, it is full of the goodness of the Son. He has patiently and graciously been working on my heart to desire Him above all. He is teaching me to trust Him and to follow His new call for my life. This change is not easy, but God and the body of Christ helps carry the weight.

Most of this past week has been like a vacation. We've been lavished with hospitality and entertained with friends and family every day. We've met new friends that we would not have otherwise known if not for this trial. I bask in the kindness of the Lord in the midst of the suffering. It's because of Christ's great love for us that he laid down his life for us and calls us his friends. As Christians, we follow suit, empowered by the Spirit to lay our lives down for others sacrificially, whether in big or small ways. We've seen church family, some of which we've hardly known, sacrifice for us in ways that our biological family would. We are different only because Jesus lives in us as Christians. None of us can love like this on our own.

One example of sacrificial and selfless love is how a family has opened up their home to us and is rearranging their house to accommodate the boys and me for up to a year without charging us anything. All of this is a gift, firstly from the giver of perfect gifts—God himself. Some things may not seem like 'gifts' at first... it was that way for me. I think partly because they often require sacrifice, humility, and challenges to some degree.

Our church family in Merlin has been an amazing pillar of support, love, and encouragement to our family. I am thankful to the Lord for all our Oregon friends and that in however a small way we could be used to help the church during the emotional transition; even if merely by being the recipients of all their love.

Now, it will be time to go home and sell many of my belongings and move from living in a four-bedroom house all to ourselves—to living with another family. The Lord has confirmed how he is going to use this new living situation to bless and sanctify us in ways we can't even imagine. The godly couple loves the children, and we enjoyed time together like one big family. I will have the opportunity to not only homeschool Noah but also work to publish a book with Josh's writings. It would not be good to be alone right now, and by God's grace for this next season, we will be able to live with a God-fearing family. I can be excited about that! I'd rather be enthralled with life than dread it with fear and weighed down with sorrow. It's another gift we have through Christ—the gift of peace and joy that is not dependent on our particular circumstances. During this trip, I have sensed confirmation to be back in LA. More sweetly, I sense a purpose and hope again in this life.

Now and then I was plagued with legalistic guilt imposed from others of needing to "prove" my love to Josh by how much I continue to lament. Then, a strong conviction from the Spirit grounded me again on what I knew to be true based on God's

Word. "Weeping may tarry for the night, but joy comes in the morning." (Psalm 30:5). My hope rested in the true assurance that my beloved was no longer in pain and suffering but in glory. Accumulating enough tears to overfill a reservoir would not burst the reality of my circumstance. It was perplexing to think why some people insisted on me staying in dark and bitter gloom. Instead, I chose to trustingly accept God's decree and celebrate my beloved's graduation into the place where I too will soon ascend. I had to stay focused on moving my boys forward and carrying on Josh's living legacy, and fighting the temptation of shrouding myself in black or camping on his grave. If I had no hope, I would have drowned myself and the children in an ocean of sorrow. It was the only option of survival. "Some people go into the furnace of affliction, and it burns them; others go in, and the experience purifies them. What makes the difference? Their attitude toward the Word of God and the will of God. If we are nourished by the Word and submit to His will, the furnace experience, painful as it may be, will refine us and make us better. But if we resist God's will and fail to feed on His truth, the furnace experience will only burn us and make us bitter." (Wiersbe, 95). I could not bear to sit in the ash heap—bitterness would have burned my heart to a crisp. Instead, I surrendered my heart to God, and in exchange He gave me hope in Christ.

Josh's solid hope was in God, through his Savior Jesus Christ. It is the same hope for those of us who have also believe in the saving name of Jesus. Many have been blessed and strengthened in the faith, as a result of sharing in the gift of Josh's life and departure from this earth. His loving memory is etched in the hearts and souls of all who have been impacted in some way by his lasting legacy. In this life, we may not know precisely why God took Josh home so young with a blossoming ministry ahead. We get a glimpse of God's purposes through all that He accomplished through His servant's short life. Moreover, we may rest in the promise of God allowing it for the good of not just our little family, but all who are His chosen people. "And we know that for those who love God all things work together for good, for those who are called according to his purpose" (Rom 8:28).

It was not merely Josh, but Christ working in his life. He was merely an instrument on loan to us. Every breath we take is borrowed, and there will come a day when our time expires, and we will have to give an account for our lives. If we do not take hold of Christ's righteousness by faith, we will stand with a dirty rap sheet to condemn us. By following Christ, we can longingly expect the day when we will be reunited with Him and all the saints in glory.

July 24, 2017

This morning as I was getting started for the day, the Lord put the hymn "Great is Thy Faithfulness" on my mind—specifically the last part of the third stanza "…strength for today and bright hope for tomorrow, blessings all mine, with ten thousand beside!" Every morning Josh taught our family to gather together to do family devotions. We usually pick out some hymns and then read scripture together. The hymn Noah picked out today was this same one the Lord had me already humming to in my head.

There are countless blessings the Lord bestows on all of us to confirm his great faithfulness and love. We've been enjoying the summer season in Oregon spending time with friends who have become very dear. Our church has truly become like a family in the short year we have spent together. The Lord has been teaching me to enjoy each day, and that joy itself becomes the strength needed.

The ministry He has for me at this present moment is mainly for my children, our home, and my Merlin church family. Some in our church tear-up when we talk about moving, and I am left bewildered. I wish things could stay the same. If only Josh were here. All I can say is this is the path the Lord would have us go now. Being close to our family will be good. I'm excited about compiling a book or two. My prayer is that many will be encouraged, and God glorified by the amazing things He has done in the life of Josh. Through his suffering and seemingly untimely death may his legacy continue. I hope you all share in my excitement and partner with us in prayer. My prayer for Merlin Church will be for the Lord to continue to do beautiful things in the upcoming years through their gracious love paired with a firm commitment to God's Word.

As I sit and ponder what our life will look like for us in the future, many hopes and dreams arise, matched with anxious thoughts. There are real fears that linger in my mind. I am trying not to let these fears surface and steal my joy. The other night I stayed up late, afraid after seeing a scorpion in my bedroom floor. I like to think the Lord gifts me with these critters in my home to give me a healthy dose of fear. Yet, God wants' me not to fear even scorpions, but only Himself. Paul says, "For me to live is Christ and to die is gain. (Phil1:21)." Without fear of our circumstances, we can truly live our lives to the fullest measure God has ordained for each of us as we live to Christ. No matter how long or how short we live, it can be well-lived if we do so selflessly, as Christ did–ready to even give up our very life out of love for our Savior and others.

Our faith is tested during the terrifying times in our life. There are times when I still weep unexpectedly—usually when I'm praying or singing songs of praise. One night, I decided to use a different Bible. I grabbed my pretty bright pink MacArthur study Bible with rose tabs. It was one that Josh had given me almost two years ago, for my 31st birthday. I stumbled upon the page where he signed it. It reads: to my beloved wife, from her eternally grateful husband. Tears started flowing, from the joy of thinking of Josh in heavenly glory reminiscing our earthly marriage with gratitude to God for all eternity.

What the Lord has used to hush my weeping is the reality that since Josh is in heaven already, there is nothing I can do to bring him back. I feel much like David when he wept and fasted before his son died and then got up and ate once he learned his baby was dead. David worshipped and when asked why, he said, "While the child was still alive, I fasted and wept for the child while he was alive; for I said, 'Who knows whether the LORD will be gracious to me, that the child may live?' But now he is dead. Why should I fast? Can I bring him back again? I shall go to him, but he will not return to me."

Josh and I together prayed and prayed along with hundreds of others who joined us in praying that God may grant him more time on this earth. We mourned together before he even went to the hospital. When Josh was in the ICU, I just kept begging God with many tears to prolong his life. As I prayed, I had to end my prayer with "Not my will, but yours be done. (Luke 22:42)" I accepted that partial healing in this life might not be God's will for Josh. I didn't doubt His wisdom. The Lord already had been training me in so many ways leading up to this point to trust in him. His grace truly does supernaturally empower us in our time of need.

He is using all of the different facets of this trial to accomplish a mighty work in our own lives and many around us.

[197]

I'm eager to continue to watch His plans unfold, and only pray that we may be filled with His wisdom, love, and Spirit to faithfully walk in what He has prepared beforehand (Eph2:10). God is in the business of resurrecting, reconciling, redeeming, restoring, recovering, returning, and regenerating. "It is quite striking that virtually all of the basic words describing salvation in the Bible imply a return to an originally good state or situation... The point of redemption is to free the prisoner from the bondage, to give back the freedom he or she once enjoyed." (*Albert Wolters, 50 Days of Heaven: Reflections That Bring Eternity to Light* by Randy Alcorn)

Great Is Thy Faithfulness

"Great is Thy faithfulness," O God my Father,
There is no shadow of turning with Thee;
Thou changest not, Thy compassions, they fail not
As Thou hast been Thou forever wilt be.
"Great is Thy faithfulness!" "Great is Thy faithfulness!"
Morning by morning new mercies I see;
All I have needed Thy hand hath provided—
"Great is Thy faithfulness," Lord, unto me!

Summer and winter, and springtime and harvest,
Sun, moon and stars in their courses above,
Join with all nature in manifold witness
To Thy great faithfulness, mercy and love.

Pardon for sin and a peace that endureth,

Thine own dear presence to cheer and to guide;

Strength for today and bright hope for tomorrow,

Blessings all mine, with ten thousand beside!

The Lord displayed His great faithfulness throughout the four years He lent us Josh. Despite the agony of walking my husband down the road of suffering and into the arms of Jesus, I count it a privilege to have been his wife. I told Josh this before he left and mean it still: "I am so thankful to God for the brief time I had with you. If I could turn back time I would not exchange these four years with you for anything!" Josh taught me so many things in such a short time. He taught me to be an excellent wife. He made me a better mom. He showed me to laugh and not take life so seriously all the time. He taught me to love, not only with words but also by his example. He taught me to be tough and not let my emotions lead my actions. Josh showed me the importance of our marriage roles. He taught me a deeper, sweeter trust in the Lord, as I learned to submit to him as my husband as unto Christ. Through Josh, God taught me also not to cling too much to our marriage but to hold it with unclenched hands. He taught me to be an encourager and to have a stronger faith. Josh showed me to be more attentive to the things in life that matter most and let the petty stuff slide, and the list goes on and on. I am eternally grateful for God giving me Josh for the season he did. Along with Job, with tested and tried faith, I can sing, "The LORD gave, and the LORD has taken away, blessed be the name of the LORD." (Job 1:21).

Josh was a true man of God, whose legacy will live on far beyond the life that he was lent here on earth. He had a tremendous godly influence on our sons Noah and Nathan, his church congregations, and everyone around him. I'm not the only one who can testify to the immense impact Josh made in his brief life. In the appendixes, you'll find testimonies from his fellow leaders and friends. This memoir is a testimony of God's grace in Josh's short, yet well-lived life. Josh's lived and died to God's glory. He exemplified Christ in His willingness to suffer and die, according to God's predetermined plan. One of his biggest concerns was for every soul to lay hold of saving faith. That is why this book ends with his plea for all to come to Christ. If you are not yet a part of God's eternal family, he would beg you to come to Christ, find a local evangelical church for corporate worship, and be eager to exalt Him together in heaven.

The Seed that the Thorns Could Not Choke Out

The sower removed his hand form the bag
Casting the seed to the ground below
Knowing that though some fell by the way
God would still cause some of it to grow

And there it lay on the sunbaked road
Where day after day it did tarry
Ripe for the ravenous appetites
Of the birds and the adversary

And some fell upon the rocky crags
Where the soil was thin as a veil
And though it did its best to spring up
The noonday heat of the sun did prevail

Still some found itself in a patch of briars
With a great thicket of thorns about

But twasn't long 'fore they lost their ground
And the thorns chocked them out

And yet we know by our Savior's words
That unless a seed die upon the ground
It can't yield an abundance of increase
And its sweet fruit cannot abound

So hung He our Savior upon the tree
Wearing a crown of thorns about
The One Who'd become the first of many
That the thorns could not choke out

Copyright Josh "J.D." Seibert

[Appendix 1]

Notes from Fellow Leaders

T
he following notes are from godly men in leadership that saw God at work through Josh. Most of these men served in leadership along-side Josh in his various ministries at different points of his life. The purpose of these testimonies' is to attest to all that God can do through a person's life surrendered to the Lord, even within a short period. They each give a snapshot of some of the journey God had Josh on before his final destination of glory. Each note is like a silver coin from the past that carries value into the future. The legacy of one dead man multiplied is like the parable of the seed that the thorns could not choke out. While Josh is physically is no longer with us, his example instills a richer life for those of us left behind. The purpose of this section is to get a snapshot of the ways Josh invested in the kingdom of heaven in different settings, seasons of life, and from different angles. As the book comes to a close, we see that the legacy that Josh left did not end with his death. Josh poured his life into the unperishable treasures of heaven, and the ripple effect of his ministry continues beyond his brief time upon this earth.

Pastor Roger Horning
Church of the Canyons, Canyon Country, CA

I've been fortunate to know Josh since he was an energetic, young 7th grader. He was attending the Youth Group at Church of the Canyons where I was the Youth Pastor. Small and squirrelly, he needed persistent supervision. Nevertheless, he was a consistent contributor to a fun atmosphere at Youth Group, and it was clear—even at 13 years old—that he genuinely cared about spiritual things. His relationship with God mattered to him, and I still remember the night he told me that he wanted to be a youth pastor when he grew up.

Josh was cool but unique. As a teen, he was well-liked by all, and his quirky personality kept people laughing. He was the lead singer and guitarist in a crazy punk band whose purpose was to reach his audience for Christ. I laughed when he would read me the lyrics to the songs (which were really good!), but I could never understand a thing during concerts when Josh was screaming the words.

It was obvious to me that the Lord had a hand on Josh's life by giving him a great love and commitment to Christ. He desired to please God and reach others with the Gospel. As Josh grew up, Colossians 3:1-2 characterized him: Therefore if you have been raised up with Christ, keep seeking the things above, where Christ is, seated at the right hand of God. Set your mind on the things above, not on the things that are on earth (NASB). Despite various difficulties and disappointments in Josh's life, he remained steadfast in seeking the things above.

Josh had many talents, but not everything came easily to him. He was a preacher, a poet, a musician, even a cowboy. Despite all of this, he struggled to find God's specific place for him—yet he faithfully pursued each God-given opportunity. He had a strong desire for marriage and parenthood, but remained faithful in his singleness into his 30s while he waited for the woman God had for him.

After spending years teaching in the public school system, he started seminary and committed his life to full-time ministry. During seminary, I watched Josh serve faithfully as a youth intern at Church of the Canyons. Again, while not everything in ministry was easy for him, he remained consistently driven by a desire to please Christ and see others come to know and love Him as their Lord.

Although things did not necessarily occur on Josh's desired time-table, God eventually granted him everything he most desired. Psalm 37:4 says, "Delight yourself in the Lord, and He will give you the desires of your heart." Expositors debate whether this passage means that God gives you what you desire or that God gives you the right desires. For Josh, God did both. His desires for ministry were noble, as was his desire for a wife and family. He wanted the right things for the right reasons.

God did eventually give Josh a wife and family. Erika was God's woman for Josh. Josh was also blessed with two wonderful sons, Noah and Nathan. While Josh loved the people to whom he ministered, his family was his priority. After seminary, he moved—first to full-time youth ministry, then to his final position as a senior pastor. In our conversations regarding the various ministry challenges he encountered, it was always clear that Josh was committed to pleasing his Master and ministering faithfully before Him. In ministry, one needs to be willing to encourage, but Josh also took the hard stand when it was required.

It was a pleasure to speak into Josh's journey and see him grow to be more effective. It never occurred to me that I would perform his funeral service, though I thought he might perform mine. There were many moments over the years where I saw Josh's commitment to the Lord, and I was inspired to be more committed. When I would listen to him preach to our youth, he stirred me to be a better preacher.

One thing I am thankful for is that he is now experiencing what he always longed for most, the presence of God. I am encouraged that I will one day see Josh again. When I do, like Josh, I will perfectly reflect the unblemished image of God.

Erika, Noah, and Nathan: I am trusting God's powerful hand of encouragement and provision in your life. I am so thankful for the three of you—for many reasons, but especially because you were the greatest earthly gift that God gave Josh.

Pastor Mike Sheridan
Community Cowboy Church, Agua Dulce, CA

Summer of 2005, Josh traveled to Northern California with me and adopted a wild mustang from the BLM which managed wild horses on the open range for the Federal Govt. After breaking him to ride, Josh showed a great interest in the horse we named "Mocha" because of his color markings. However, one day Josh was careless getting off Mocha and caught his spur in the horse's mane. As a result, Mocha moved quickly and dumped Josh on the ground, causing his arm to become broken. His mom came and took him to the hospital where they set the arm in a cast. Josh was never able to regain full mobility of that arm from that time on. But it never stopped him from writing a poem about that incident and many others after that. I think Josh felt that his injury just proved he was a cowboy after all.

As Josh's riding ability improved, he wanted more authentic

cowboy experiences. So when a rancher friend of mine in Nevada called and wanted help at the roundup and branding time, a bunch of us went up and took Josh with us. He pitched right in and did his part of rounding up the cattle and holding them at branding time. Once again, his horse of choice was Mocha.

Besides our riding and cowboy type activities, Josh also helped with our hometown Church ministry. Another summer we went to the High Sierras with several church families and camped at Whitsett Lake. I asked Josh how deep it was and he decided to jump in and head for the bottom. He found out it was ten feet deep and offered no problem supporting our canoes. He also played music for our kids Sunday school and even drove our pony and cart in the local parade with our Church banner on the cart. Throughout the years, we had fun together and used these experiences to minister the Word to others as well.

Adam Holland
Deacon, Crossroads Community Church, Valencia, CA

Friendships can take on a variety of forms; some are more like acquaintances, others are more like family, while some are not lengthy over time, but are deep in meaning.

I first met Josh at a post-college Bible study at Grace Baptist Church. In the group, he always showed great care and compassion for the variety of people and stories the group presented and shared his great love of the Lord, cowboys, and the West with us all. We were more acquaintances in the small group, but two things would happen in our lives that would make us friends.

While in the young adult group we were both pursuing teaching credentials in history. We often talked about the educational process, what we loved about people, and how we wanted to change people's lives through teaching. We started our teaching careers at different schools, but often checked-in with each other to see how it was going, and Josh extended great encouragement as we both "survived" our first year.

Josh would later leave teaching to go to seminary, and we would lose contact as he completed seminary and went into full-time ministry in Arizona and Oregon. During that time, we were more acquaintances and to be honest, do not remember any specific contact or conversation.

In 2014 I was diagnosed with brain cancer and Josh, and I rekindled a friendship, and he wrote that he was praying for me, which he truly meant. So many of us, including myself, often say that we'll be praying, but forget or don't mean it. Josh was a man of his word, and what he said, he did. During our communications, Josh proudly talked about his wife, family, church, and was so thankful for the path the Lord had him on.

We wouldn't talk again until a couple of years later after I had written a book, Anchored in the Storm, a devotional for those suffering. Josh had been diagnosed with MDS and Erika had bought him my book. Our friendship was renewed as we discussed God's purpose in suffering and the mighty things God would do through Josh, his testimony, and the impact Josh's story will have on the lives of his family, his churches, and the Christian community. We talked a few times before his passing, and each conversation was encouraging as they were when I first met Josh. He continued to be kind, generous, and always with humor throughout.

Josh's passing surprised me, but it didn't surprise the Lord whom he fervently served. Josh was always eager to please the Lord and throughout our friendship exhibited his excitement to see what God was going to do through him whether as a cowboy, teacher, seminary student, pastor, husband, and now a wonderful memory.

He left a beautiful legacy of poems and sermons that will encourage all towards a greater love of Christ, and the West too!

Pastor John Chester
Piedmont Bible Church, Haymarket, Virginia

I met Josh on my first day of seminary. In fact, I met him first thing in the morning on the first day of seminary; we were seated at the same table for the first session of our week-long orientation. That was the first of countless times we sat at the same table while we were in seminary. We almost always ate lunch together and often sat next to each other in class (in the front row). Although after seminary, as the demands of ministry and life mounted, our contact dwindled to seeing each other at conferences and a few phone calls a year, we were fast friends, having formed a friendship that will last an eternity.

One of the best things about our friendship was seeing the Lord at work in one another's lives. It was indeed a privilege to see how God was working in Josh's life. I'm a few years older than Josh, and we very naturally fell into an older/younger brother dynamic, so I was always overjoyed to see the Lord at work in his life and for him to grow.

Nowhere did he grow more and more evidence the working of the Lord in his life than how he grew in communicating the truth of God's Word to people. Josh was hit with a double whammy that was getting in his way. He was a quirky guy that some people might misread as awkward and aloof, and he was very, very smart, so smart that even when he tried to simplify things, he could often speak about the deep things of God in a way that many found hard to follow. He was a complex thinker trying to express complex thoughts, and sometimes there is no simple way to do that.

These things came together and created a crisis for Josh near the end of our seminary career. After completing the preaching lab, a rite of passage at TMS, Josh was told he had to take another supplemental preaching lab, it was for those students whom the professors felt were not ready to preach a Sunday sermon to the actual flock of an actual church. Josh was crestfallen even though he said he had been expecting it.

Having never heard Josh preach (I had been in a different lab) and wanting to encourage and support him, I audited his first sermon in the supplemental lab. I don't remember his text, but I remember feeling like I should have had a bidder's paddle because he wasn't so much preaching as delivering information with the unbreathing rapidity of an auctioneer. It was a little hard to watch because I knew his warm-hearted passion for the glory of God and his love for God's people, and none of that was reflected in his preaching.

When we talked about it he told me that he was so used to people not wanting to listen to him that he just wanted to get it all out while they were still listening. I think this fear grew out of two of the things that made Josh, Josh. First Josh was a cowboy, not the kind who wore a Stetson while driving his pickup truck to go line dancing, but the kind that actually rode a horse and worked cattle (and even wrote cowboy poetry); Josh was more confident reading the reactions of animals than he was reading people. Secondly, Josh loved conspiracy theories, and he loved to share them with others. Even now I'm not entirely sure how much he believed and how much the mischievous storyteller in him just enjoyed spinning a great yarn.

Apparently, he had perceived that people would tune him out about halfway through things like his compelling case for how the U.S. Forest Service was suppressing the evidence for Sasquatch. He became a little gun shy, so he spoke too fast even when preaching.

Over the next year, the Lord taught him a powerful lesson that he shared with me. It's not Josh who people needed to listen to; it was the word of God's truth that he was speaking that was important. Then something amazing happened; Josh slowed down. As the Lord worked in his life he was transformed from someone who was convinced that no one would listen to him so he had to get it all out at once, to someone convicted that no one needed to listen to him, but that they needed to hear about his Savior, so he slowed down. Josh went from someone who needed a remedial preaching class to being a clear and powerful communicator of God's Word.

That is just one of the many things I was blessed to see the Lord do in Josh's life. There was never a time it wasn't apparent that God was at work in and through Josh. When I think of heaven one of the things I long for is another opportunity to sit at the same table with Josh; to talk, laugh and pray together. Praise be to God, we will have an eternity of those opportunities on the new earth.

Pastor Austin Duncan
Grace Community Church, Sun Valley, CA

Some years ago, I attended a banquet for local pastors hosted by a crisis pregnancy center. A young woman spoke at the banquet and shared her testimony of faith in Christ and what a blessing it was to choose to keep her baby. I silently prayed for her, thanked God for her faith and asked that he would provide a Godly husband for her and a father for her son Noah. I met Erika briefly after the banquet and found out she attended our church.

Josh was a single seminarian when I first met him, a "bachelor buckaroo." He was an answer to the prayers of so many in our church, when he met and married Erika. Every time I saw their young family at church I was reminded of God's kind providence in bringing these two together. And as God added another son,

Nathan, to their family they experienced the joy and blessing of God in their lives. When Josh was called to pastor first in Arizona and later in Oregon, we knew they would be missed. Their family packed up, with no idea that a storm would soon break.

I closely followed the Seibert's agonizing trial online, and we continued to pray for them. A young family, a growing church and a difficult disease. God's grace was apparent as they endured affliction, bore their cross, and trusted in their heavenly Father not knowing his inscrutable ways. When God called Josh to himself, it was devastating for all who knew and loved him. His friends, his beloved church, his boys and his precious wife all experienced agonizing sorrow but held closely to their faith. As the years have passed the sovereignty of God continues to give comfort to the bereaved, and Josh's life continues to provide a testimony to God's faithfulness.

Josh Seibert was a cowboy, a poet and a pastor. What makes a real cowboy isn't the hat or the belt buckle. A real cowboy has an ability to work a herd, to care for his horse and ride through adversity. This was Josh. He represented the old way, the cowboy way. A toughness in adversity that kept him humbly enduring his painful trial dependent on Christ.

Josh Seibert was also J.D. Seibert, the cowboy poet. He had a real gift for weaving words to make a memorable verse. His poems were published in magazines and he performed his spoken words at festivals. My favorite line is from a unique poem that combines his love of the West with his theology of Christ's return:

> Now, the boss ain't slow in comin'
> As some may count slowness to be
> He's just lookin' to build a herd
> That will last for eternity

Josh was also a pastor. Working with young people in southern California and Arizona he was a faithful evangelist and shepherd. When he was called to shepherd the church in Oregon, he faithfully answered that call. Josh's ministry to his church was brief but biblical, short term but with an eternal testimony. Josh will be remembered as a faithful pastor, real cowboy, winsome poet, loving father, and devoted husband. But above all his testimony of trust points to his Savior and God who cares for His flock perfectly, shepherd's his people patiently, and speaks comfort to us in poetic language like this:

Who can speak and have it happen

If the Lord has not decreed it?

Is it not from the mouth of the Most High

That both calamities and good things come?

Lamentations 3:37-38

Though he brings grief, he will show compassion,

So great is his unfailing love.

For he does not willingly bring affliction

Or grief to the children of men.

Lamentations 3:32-33

May Josh's ministry and testimony continue to help us to live in light of eternity!

Pastor Michael Mahoney
Grace Community Church, Sun Valley, CA

As a pastor at Grace Community Church, I am blessed to meet many seminary students preparing to be involved in full-time ministry. Josh Seibert was one of them, and in many ways, one in a thousand of them. He was a uniquely gifted man who could walk into the room and fill everyone's hearts with joy. His friendly, compassionate heart touched everyone who came in contact with him. Someone once said, "You make a living by what you get; you make a life by what you give." Josh made a life by giving joy to his friends and family, and the hope of the gospel to the lost. I am one of the many grateful witnesses of Josh's profoundly impactful friendship.

Memories fade with time. But not memories that capture distinct solemnity. I had the privilege of officiating Josh and Erika's wedding ceremony. Oh, how he loved Erika! He wanted to honor Christ and please Him in every aspect of the ceremony. The wedding put on display his passion for the gospel and his profound love for His Savior. Their wedding will always remain in my memory as one that most exalted the Lord Jesus Christ—it is really a memory that is consistent with all of Josh's life. As Proverbs 10:7 says, "The memory of the righteous is blessed."

Josh's love for his Savior and his bride did not end at the wedding; he faithfully demonstrated it throughout his life. He took his role of exemplifying Christ in their marriage seriously. He grew in his love for Erika throughout their marriage. He also quickly learned to be a kind and caring father to his children. The Lord had special favor on him in all of this, perhaps because He knew Josh only had a short time on earth.

Josh was a pastor at heart even when he came to seminary before his pastorate. He was serious about his calling to shepherd's Christ's body. It did not mean that he was serious in his demeanor; he had a great sense of humor that enabled him to approach seminary, marriage, fatherhood, pastorate, and all of life with a joyful attitude because he knew he served Christ in everything he did. What more can be said of anyone's life? These are the kinds of things people say about someone who has lived a full life into their seventies and eighties. But, in a way, Josh did live a full life even in its brevity because he lived in light of eternity, where he now beholds his Savior face to face.

Jason Metcalf

Former Deacon at College Park Baptist Church, Prescott, Arizona

I saw the impact of the Lord using Josh with the youth, others, and me. Josh's impact with the youth started at College Park, but it went beyond that at The Merge gatherings and camps. His love for the Lord and the value he placed on teaching the Word and sharing the gospel was an answer to many prayers. Solid teaching and the gospel was missing at the youth group. The Christian students weren't growing, and the unsaved weren't hearing the gospel.

Josh's background as a high school teacher prior to seminary allowed him to connect quickly with the youth. He knew how to communicate at their level and he not only shared the gospel with them, but he shared his life. His teaching was intense, yet it was funny and entertaining too. He used clever illustrations to remind us of God's truths. I will never forget his mistake of throwing a skunk's scent gland in a vacant field next to his house. The whole neighborhood near the field was filled with that rank skunk smell, but Josh was able to use the incident as an illustration about how odious sin is to God and how he wants us to be a sweet odor. I saw many young people strengthened in their faith or come to faith through Josh's faithful sharing of the gospel.

His ministry went beyond the church walls. He would go to the schools and meet in the teen Bible clubs to bring encouragement to their walks. Some of the teenagers in the youth group were in rebellion, and Josh lovingly disciplined them and prayed for them. One of those teens was my son. He wasn't living for Jesus and got into some trouble his senior year, but God used Josh's passing and other events to bring him into His fold. The impact of some of the kids' lives has been seen posthumously, but I know Josh would have been blessed to know that the prodigals have come home. His life had an impact because he loved the kids and unabashedly lived the gospel in front of the youth, so they all knew where he stood and where he went upon leaving this world.

He had an impact on others too. I know many people who were touched by his life and ministry. I saw many church members who were sad and weeping when Josh departed for Oregon to be a senior pastor. They missed his kind, soft spirit. He was always ready to pray for a need and to encourage others. I saw this even toward the end of his life shortly after his radiation therapy and on the day of his transplant. Before having the transplant, we walked the halls of his unit, and he was encouraging the family members and patients on the unit and offering prayers for them. In his time of greatest struggle (a literal fight for his life), like Jesus, he was focused on others and shared the gospel and Christ's love. I saw people "light up" when Josh would talk with them even though he was very sick. He even encouraged and shared the gospel with hospital staff. I was blessed to see his impact on others while in Kingman and his last days.

Josh also impacted me. I was first introduced to Josh by viewing a final sermonette he had delivered at the Master's Seminary. College Park Church was looking for a new youth pastor, and I was helping screen candidates. Josh's teaching was solid and captivating, and I believed Josh would be the right pastor for the youth. I had a chance to meet him for the first time when the church requested that he and Erika come for an interview and visit. Josh and I were about the same height, and we connected immediately. I didn't realize at that time how much of a friend and dear brother he would become. When he started in the youth group, he quickly removed anything that distracted from a healthy environment for youth to worship and hear the Word. We were like-minded in ministry perspectives, and we loved serving together. We didn't just serve together though, we became friends. We took our boys fishing together and spent countless hours talking about theology and life in general. I felt honored to be his reference for pastoral positions he sought when he felt that time had come. When he got the role in Oregon, I was excited at the thought of being able to see him during the summers because I had lived in Oregon before moving to Kingman. God had different plans though.

I remember in December 2016 getting a phone call from Josh asking for my thoughts about a call he received from OHSU asking him to have some tests done and possible treatment for a medical condition I had never heard of. I was concerned because the medical care could be expensive, but I was also concerned because they called him. Before moving to Oregon, I had worked at the University of Washington Medical Center. I knew that one doesn't get a call from an academic medical center unless the person is a "special case." In my flesh, I didn't want him to go, but he knew he had to do everything he could to be around for his family. He had to fight for his life. I never had a chance to hang out with Josh in Oregon outside a hospital. I went through the grief steps like many others when Josh went home. I experienced denial, anger, bargaining with God, depression, and finally acceptance. I miss him even today, but I know that he can say like Paul, "I have fought the good fight, I have finished the race, I have kept the faith. Henceforth there is laid up for me the crown of righteousness, which the Lord, the righteous judge, will award to me on that day, and not only me but also to all who loved his appearing" (2 Timothy 4:7-8 English Standard Version). I look forward to the day we will meet again in the presence of our Savior.

Dr. Jason Allen

Teacher/Deacon at College Park Baptist Church, Kingman, Arizona

When remembering Josh, the parable of the sheep and the goats in Matthew 25 comes to mind. Josh never met a stranger and was always ready to share whatever he could in a material way. He was quick to follow up with sharing the Gospel no matter the setting. I recall one day during the middle of the week when I received a call from Josh at my podiatry practice. He was calling from outside our local Walmart where he and a couple of other men from the church had been sharing the Gospel to whomever the Lord brought their way. In one particular case, they had befriended a gentleman that was apparently of little means, possibly homeless. Josh wanted a little medical advice from me regarding how best to care for this man's feet, as they were physically in bad shape. Josh intended to take him back to the church to clean up his feet and care for them, making sure they provided for his physical needs to address his spiritual needs. All of this was to demonstrate the love of Christ tangibly. I have not met many in my lifetime who have been so ready and willing not only to demonstrate Christ's love but to do it in such an extravagant way. Josh was a truly remarkable man of God who allowed the love of Christ to flow through him in order to reach a lost world. Josh was a man who loved to study and preach the Word of God faithfully. But more than that, he lived out what Christ has called all of us to do, and that is to go into all the world and preach the gospel to the whole creation.

Pastor Peter A. Ernst

Family Bible Church, Kingman, Arizona

Josh Siebert was one of those special people you meet in your life where you immediately see the hand of God in them and on them. Josh was a faithful man of God who most definitely had the call of God on His life. Josh had an obvious anointing through gifts of preaching, leading, Biblical knowledge and the wisdom that comes through walking with God in the power of the Holy Spirit. Josh had a pastor's / shepherd's heart as he longed to see his wife (Erika) and his beloved children, youth group and church family come to spiritual maturity in Jesus Christ.

Josh met with four faithful, godly men of the same mind and heart every Friday morning as together we pursued the doctrines of grace, meeting together for Biblical discipleship and mutual accountability. We wrestled together in coming to understand the majesty, beauty and sovereign providence of God the Father, God the Son and God the Holy Spirit. Every Friday morning, we enjoyed clean fun, laughter, and banter as men but also, we would pursue subjects of relevance of the day and needs of our lives. We immediately saw integrity in Josh, a man of sterling character and Christ-like values, a man who was striving to become wholly holy. It was our privilege to watch him, sit under his wisdom and share alongside him the walk of faith, as friends and as partners in the work of ministry. When Josh told us he was leaving the area to pursue his own pastorate, we rejoiced and thought it time, for Josh showed remarkable maturity beyond his years. We were crushed in spirit to hear of his illness and faithfully partnered with him in prayer until the Lord took him to his reward.

Even now, as I reflect on what God did in Josh, what God did through Josh and what God has done in us, I am once again thankful for the providence of Almighty God who sees the end from the beginning and everything in between. What a comfort to know God knows us and sent His Son to be the propitiation for our sins. Having the privilege of knowing Josh has made all of us richer and better people. It is ultimately Christ in us that is our hope of glory!

Dr. David W. Hegg
Senior Pastor, Grace Baptist Church, Santa Clarita, CA

Josh Seibert was a very bright young man, with a great heart for Christ and the church. I had the privilege of conversing him on several occasions as he encountered challenges in ministry. He appreciated my years of experience and often turned to me and other trusted counselors for advice. I was particularly impressed with his ability to see through the chaff to the core of the challenge and recognize the short and long term consequences of making a hasty decision. Josh always made the most of his education and was on the way to be a great pastoral leader when God called him home. Yet, even in his last years, he maintained an attitude of joy that I will always remember. We're all better off for having had Josh in our lives.

Pastor Jake Tromburg
South Norfolk Christian Church, Chesapeake, VA

I first met Josh at TMS and liked him right away. He was open and honest, and not afraid to speak his mind. One of the things that struck me about Josh initially was his sincerity. He truly had a pastor's heart and seemed to welcome anyone without pretense. He also had a broad range of unique interests that always made conversations interesting!

After I graduated, he had married Erika, and we went our separate ways but would catch up as our paths crossed. I knew the transition was difficult, and it was a blessing to spend some time with him in the midst of that and hear him share his heart. It was clear his concern wasn't for himself, but for the people God had called him to minister to. I rejoiced with him to hear about the church he had been called to, and I knew they would be blessed. I'm thankful for Josh. I'm thankful for his sincerity, and for how serious he was about his calling as a minister of the gospel, and I know he is now rejoicing in the light he only saw dimly here on earth.

Pastor Ken Drake
Clackamas Bible Church, Portland, OR

On February 1, 2017, a lady in our church received a prayer request from the Luis Palau Organization. The request was from Kim Seibert on behalf of her son Josh who was in need of housing in March and April. Josh was to have a bone marrow transplant and his wife, Erika, and sons Noah and Nathan would stay near Oregon Health Sciences University Hospital in Portland, Oregon for the procedure and follow-up care time. A call was made, and the lady who received the request offered her home. This need was made known to the Board of Clackamas Bible Church, and a decision was made to allow Josh and his family, along with a friend and nanny named Katelynn to stay in a duplex owned by the church. This 3-bedroom duplex was located next to the church and provided a place for them to stay.

As pastor of the church, I first met with Josh and Erika in March to show them the duplex and to invite them to be part of our church family. Although Josh was in the hospital for a lot of the time during their stay, the family was able to participate in Wednesday night dinners and other church events. Noah was sad about missing out on AWANA at his church in Merlin, but he quickly became a part of our AWANA and immediately fit right in. The family was invited to several homes for meals and over time got to know many of the people in our church. The Seiberts stayed in the duplex until Josh passed away in the summer of 2017.

In my short time knowing Josh, there were a couple of things that stood out to me. The first thing was the care and concern he showed towards his wife and two boys. It was very difficult to know that his time on this earth might be short and that he would be leaving Erika and the boys behind. He was an amazing husband and father to his family. As a church family, we wanted Josh to know that we would step in and provide some help while he was in the hospital and recovering.

I only had the opportunity to meet with Josh in the duplex and the hospital on a couple of occasions. However, the second thing that impressed me was Josh's faith. Hebrews 11:1 tells us "Now faith is confidence in what we hope for and assurance about what we do not see." Josh exhibited this kind of faith in his words and his actions. I remember sitting with him in his hospital room on one occasion and being amazed at how much peace he had despite his situation. It was one of those times where I went to encourage an individual and lift their spirits and left being encouraged myself. We talked together of what it meant to be a pastor of a church and the joy of being able to lead people in their walk with the Lord. We spoke of God's love and the truth of God's Word and the privilege of preaching and teaching it to others. Josh had faith. He was confident that what he believed about God was true and that even though he could not see it, he could trust it.

Hebrews 11:1 is the opening sentence of the great chapter on faith. It is often referred to as the Hall of Faith. It speaks of the examples of faith in Scripture from creation to the time of Christ. People like Abraham, Moses, and Elijah who believed God and follow Him in faith. I believe that this Hall of Faith is not a closed list. Names are being added daily to the list as people trust God and go to be with Him. I know for certain that if we were to update the list of the Hall of Faith, we would see the name of Josh Seibert listed there. His faith impacted people while he was here – his family and friends, people at the churches where he served, and all the other people that he met. His faith impacted me. I see this same kind of faith in his wife, Erika. Josh was and is a man of faith. The only change is that now his faith has become sight as he enjoys fellowship for all eternity with God the Father, Son, and Holy Spirit and all of those who believe in the Lord Jesus Christ.

[Appendix 2]

Becoming a "Christian" or a Disciple of Jesus

So you've heard many things, and you find yourself asking, "OK, so what do I do with all of this?" If you feel that God is opening your heart to come to know Him you need to do two things, 1) Repent from your sins and 2) Place your faith in Jesus. Here's what the Bible says about how you can be "saved" and have peace with God by becoming a disciple of Jesus. Please read the following verses and recognize and respond.

Recognize:

- God is your Creator and Owner (Psalm 24:1)
- You have been born a sinner (Romans 3:23; 5:12)
- All sin is a direct rebellion against God (1 John 3:4-6)
- Because you sin you stand to receive eternal punishment in Hell (Romans 6:23; 1 Corinthians 6:9-11)
- You are a sinner in need of a Savior (John 12:47; Luke 19:10)
- God has supplied Jesus to save the world from its sin (John 1:29; 1 John 4:14-15)

Respond:

- You need to pray to God, asking Him to forgive your sins based upon what Jesus did for you on the cross (Acts 2:38; 26:20;)
- Believe in the Person, Sayings and Miracles of Jesus as King of Your life (Acts 16:31)

- Ask God to give you His Holy Spirit to help enable you to live the Christian life and reveal to you the truth about Jesus (John 15:26)

If you have recognized what the Bible says about you and God and your need for salvation in Jesus for the first time, please let someone know so that they can encourage you in your new faith and teach you about what your new decision means. Also, make sure that you get plugged into a church so that you can learn what it means to be a disciple of Jesus! Congratulations!

Grace and Peace,
Josh Seibert

Bibliography

Cuyler, Theodore. *God's Light on Dark Clouds*. 1882. Carlisle: The Banner of Truth, 2008.

Elliot, Elisabeth. *The Path of Loneliness*. 1998. Grand Rapids: Revell, 2007.

Fitzpatrick, Elyse. *A Steadfast Heart*. Phillipsburg: P&R Publishing Company, 2006.

Furman, Dave. *Being There*. Wheaton: Lifeway, 2016.

---, *Kiss the Wave*. Wheaton: Lifeway, 2018.

Holland, Adam. *Anchored in the Storm*. San Bernardino, 2016.

Kovacs, Gabor T, Sue A Breheny, Melinda J Dear. "Embryo donation at an Australian university in-vitro fertilization clinic: issues and outcomes." Wiley Online Library, 2003. https://onlinelibrary.wiley.com/doi/abs/10.5694/j.1326-5377.2003.tb05103.x. Accessed on 10 April, 2019.

Lawson, Steve. *Hollman Old Testament Commentary: Psalm 1-75*. Nashville: Broadman & Holman Publishers, 2003.

MacArthur, John. *The Power of Suffering*. Wheaton: Victor Books, 1995.

Piper, John, and Justin Taylor. *Suffering and the Sovereignty of God*. Wheaton: Crossway, 2006.

Wiersbe, Warren W. *Be Patient*. 1991. Colorado Springs: Victor, 2004.

Acknowledgments

Friends and family, you have propelled the birth of this book and helped shape its course. Thank you for your enthusiasm, support, and prayers during the past two years. You kept me going during those times when I had enough tears and emotional toll from re-living memories of Josh, and just wanted to be done with it. You instilled wisdom and patience for me to preserve and take my time to allow God to do a perfect work through it. A special thank you to Marie Tromburg, Teri White, Megan Gaske, the Sandoval family, and Don & Kim Seibert for your love and support.

Merlin Community Baptist Church, you poured your love on Josh and our family in such a way that gives much glory to God who can only empower it from His Spirit within you. Instead of dismissing Josh and sending our family packing, you embraced us even more after hearing the news of his diagnosis. You filled the minds of unbelievers with awe at the tangible display of Christ-like love and answer to prayer for financial provisions. A special acknowledgment to Mike Friend, LaGina Skalley, Dwight Bolen, Larry Crawl, and all the elders for going the extra mile. Thank you Margo Bartow, for being the faithful friend I could call at any hour of the night, and for your ongoing encouragement of my writing. Thank you Linda Slade, for your motherly affection and willingness to sleep on my couch to comfort my aching heart.

Grace Community Church, thank you for your kindness in partnering with us in prayer when you got news of Josh's disease and passing. Thank you to the elders for your prayers and support. Thank you Pastor Michael Mahoney for the flowers and condolences. Thank you to everyone at The Master's Seminary for the special tribute to Josh during the 31st Commencement Ceremony. Thank you Pastor John MacArthur for your willingness to help with the book, which was of great motivation to press on. Thank you Dr. Steve Lawson for your commitment to preach the word, and to tell the stories the faithful saints who have gone before us. It was such an encouragement for me in this endeavor. Thank you Dr. Al Mohler for your faith in the power of God through an unknown minister such as my husband.

Church of the Canyons, thank you for being supportive throughout Josh's life and death. You generously supported us during the times we needed it most. You all showered us with love on our wedding and likewise the day of Josh's memorial service. Thank you to each of you who helped put together a God-honoring marriage ceremony, and gospel-centered memorial service. A special thanks to Pastor Rodger Horning, Daniel and Stephanie Castillo, and Yolanda Daniels.

College Park Baptist Church, thank you for your forever friendships and support of Josh's ministry. A heartfelt acknowledgment to Jerry & Belinda Cook who became our adoptive parents in the Lord. Thank you Rob and Tracy Sawyer for your willingness to help in any way, even in lending us your daughter for a few months. A big thank you to Katelynn Sawyer for your love and care of the boys while Josh was in the hospital. Also, thank you to Brian and Kay Williams for your support to our family and in the youth ministry. A fond acknowledgment to our youth staff, Dani Kregler, Jason Metcalf, Sam Wells, David and Joylynn DeFord, Jonathan Nicolos, and Deborah Goreham. Thank you church body for your generous financial offering and your faithful prayers.

Clackamas Bible Church, thank you for being part of the beautiful story of God's provision for our family in Portland. Josh was so relieved that the boys and I would have spiritual and emotional support while he was hospitalized. Thank you Pastor Ken, for your spiritual ministry and your friendship with our entire family, especially Noah. Thank you Bonnie Watzig for always checking on us and making sure we had all we needed. Thank you to the church body for the meals, cards, and party invitations that meant so much to us.

Thank you, John Chester for your excellent resources and pointing me to the right people for help. Eric Dodson, thank you for your thorough job editing the first draft of the book, and generously giving your time and expertise. John Manning, thank you for your professionalism with editing and formatting. Stephen Melniszyn, thank you for seeing my vision for the cover and prayerfully crafting the perfect design for this book.

Thank you to the authors, pastors and professionals that showed me the ropes on how to make this book dream a reality, especially Adam Holland, Nathan Pickowicz, and Linda Killian. Thanks to everyone who took the time to proofread my book: Pastor Paul Twiss, Ashley Currie, and Marie Tromburg.

Thank you to the men who contributed a written essay, for the treasured gift of getting a better glimpse of the immeasurable impact of one man's life wholly surrendered to God's work: Dr. William Varner, Pastor Roger Horning, Adam Holland, Pastor John Chester, Pastor Mike Sheridan, Pastor Michael Mahoney, Pastor Austin Duncan, Jason Metcalf, Dr. Jason Allen, Pastor Peter Ernst, Dr. David Hegg, Pastor Jake Tromburg, and Pastor Ken Drake. Without the encouragement of you all, this would not have been possible.

About the Author

Erika Seibert was born and raised in Southern California to a large family in Los Angeles. She is the oldest of five—three sisters and a brother. Her hobbies include spending time with family and friends, traveling, hiking, reading, blogging, studying the Bible, and scrapbooking. Her love for God's Word led her to pursue an MA in Biblical Studies from The Master's University. Erika served alongside her late husband Josh Seibert in youth and pastoral ministry. Josh graduated from

The Master's Seminary in 2013. Erika has two energetic boys, Noah and Nathan, who love to socialize and keep active in sports. She is passionate about the Lord, her two children, writing, and using her own journey to encourage others.

Made in the USA
San Bernardino, CA
09 March 2020